Praise for T

This book will transform how you lead is practical and powerful for maintaining your optimum health, so you own your power and bring your best self forward.

Jack Canfield, Coauthor of the New York Times *Bestselling* Chicken Soup for the Soul® *series and* The Success Principles: How to Get from Where You Are to Where You Want to Be™

Cate's dynamic personality emanates through her writing. She provides the reader with universal tools to create strength and confidence in the workplace as well as in life outside the office. *The Powerhouse in You* will really help you dig into why you are like you are, why you do what you do and gives you the tools to change those things that you feel need changing.

Carol Petryschuk, MS, RD

Cate Collins is a master coach, mentor and storyteller. She effortlessly becomes your confidante through the pages, sharing wisdom and insights thoughtfully and thought-provokingly, encouraging the reader to become their very best self for themselves first, and then for what they can give to the world. Gentle but determined, she plumbs the psyche and the soul to release the inner leader in all of us and fuels that leader with her no-nonsense truth. Thank you Cate for helping me tap into my powerhouse!

Noel Coppins, Owner and CMO, RE/MAX Jazz Inc., brokerage

Cate Collins challenges us to embrace our power as we tackle life and leadership. *The Powerhouse in You* couldn't have come to me at a better time, when my life changed in the blink of an eye through an unexpected family crisis. …Cate inspired me to own my power by prioritizing my health, wellness and self-care, as I respond to the needs of others. She reminded me to pause to put on my own oxygen mask so I can be strong, fit, and confident as I navigate the changes going on around me. I recommend this book to all who aspire to be healthier, resilient people and better leaders.

Terri Gray, Executive Director, Community Living Oshawa

You must read this book ASAP. Cate speaks to you, to your heart and soul about servant leadership and self-care and work-life balance. I learned so many critical lessons – the first lesson being, take care of yourself. You'll want to absorb every word.

Kathy Cargile, Senior Analyst – Strategy American Airlines Cargo

Cate delivers exactly what the world needs right now – a toolkit of advice, tricks and tips for human survival and leadership. Cate delivers a powerful message in a compelling, genuine, impactful way – perfectly balancing business skills with spirituality. This book is one that will resonate with people of every age, background and experience level. The simplicity and memorability of the four-room metaphor really stuck. A must read for every current and future leader.

Trish Paterson, CEO, Copper Branch

Cate Collins hits it on the nail! This book arrived in my life exactly at the time I needed it! I was hooked with the statement, "*The Powerhouse in You* is about owning your power and connecting with the powerhouse leader in you!" And I kept on turning the pages. Each chapter brought a great sense of clarity to me; the exercises provided opportunities to recall profound examples of leadership from the past and present. The imperative for taking charge of my destiny has become a driving force.

The key takeaway and lesson is for leaders to be clear on where to draw our lines, particularly as it relates to our wellness. There is hope and strategies we can use regardless of the choices we make. This book is a lovely mirror for leaders – it will make you reflect and act!

Dr. Karima Velji, RN, PhD, CHE, Vice President Clinical Services, Ontario Shores Centre for Mental Health Sciences

Who better than Cate Collins, a Powerhouse herself, to inspire, encourage and empower you to live your best life. You'll want to read *The Powerhouse in You* with highlighter and note pad in hand. It will be constantly by my side to help me support others' leadership journeys, as well as my own. Thank you Cate for sharing your wisdom!

Nicola Crow, Executive Director, Durham Family Court

Many in today's world are feeling isolated, particularly in the wake of a pandemic. ... a fantastic reminder on the importance of leaders remaining present, and maintaining meaningful connections to remain focused and inspired.

Natalie Prychitko, CEO, Whitby Chamber of Commerce

Cate Collins' *The Powerhouse in You* is an excellent guide for all leaders. A leader herself, Cate takes you on a journey to discover your resilience, courage and confidence and opens doors to the four rooms full of discovery. If you are a leader or long to be one, your quest is about to begin.

Nancy Shaw, CEO, Greater Oshawa Chamber of Commerce

Wow! Cate's book is an excellent read. It will help you discover and know that: You matter, You are worthy and You deserve to find inner peace. Through her exercises she will help you to interpret and build on your four rooms, leading you to the discovery of your true self and your inner peace. A great book for leaders, yet also for anyone who is trying to find their calm and their inner strength. I wish I had read this when I was in business.

Laurel Armstrong, Happily Retired, Past Director at Scotia Wealth Management (a division of Scotia Capital and Scotiabank)

Cate Collins has done an outstanding job at passionately creating a manual to awaken the powerhouse leader in all of us. This book has brought together deceptively simple practices that address the balance of mind, body and spirit which can transform the consciousness of humanity. I recommend *The Powerhouse in You* to everyone who wants to become a better version of themselves and a better leader of others.

Michael Coulas, D.C., Owner of Awakened Life Chiropractic and Wellness Centre

THE
POWERHOUSE
IN YOU

How to lead
with greater
resilience,
courage and
confidence

CATE COLLINS

Copyright © 2020 by Cate Collins

All rights reserved. No part of this publication may be reproduced, transmitted or stored in any form or by any means without the prior written permission of the author.

The information contained in this book is a collection of research, training, experience, participating in seminars, books, and the many clients that the author has had the honour to work with. Due to the complexity of and the continual changes occurring in the subject matter, the author cannot be held responsible for errors or omissions, or consequences of any actions resulting from information in this book. Examples discussed are intended as general guidelines only. If acknowledgment for someone's work has been inadvertently missed, the author extends sincere apologies. Names and characters bearing any resemblance to real persons or events is purely coincidental.

This book is intended to support the reader however is not a substitute for therapy or medical advice. The author disclaims all responsibility for any liability or risk that is incurred as a consequence, directly or indirectly, from the use and application of any of the content in this book.

ISBN (paperback): 978-1-7773675-0-3
ISBN (e-book): 978-1-7773675-1-0
ISBN (audiobook): 978-1-7773675-2-7

Edited by: Catherine Leek of Green Onion Publishing
Interior Design and Layout by: Kim Monteforte of Kim Monteforte Graphic Design Services
Cover Design by: Azadeh Yaraghi of Gogo Telugo Creatives

In honour of my sister-law-in, Mary Callipo,
who passed away of cancer during COVID-19.

Your free spirit lives on in each of
our hearts to remind us to laugh more,
play more, and definitely dance more.

Contents

Awakening Your Power 1

Chapter 1 WHAT'S POWER GOT TO DO WITH BEING
A LEADER? 5
    A Typical Struggle for Power 6
    Accepting Powerlessness 7
    Have You Given Your Power Away? 8
    Have You Robbed Someone of Their Power? 13

Chapter 2 WHAT DOES IT MEAN TO BE A POWERHOUSE? 17
    Finding Your Powerhouse Qualities 18
    Your Powerhouse and the Four Rooms 19
    Becoming a Powerhouse. 21

Room One
Your Mentally Fit Room

Chapter 3 MENTAL BLIND SPOTS 25
    Distorted Belief System. 25
    Fear-Based Narratives. 26
    Your Limiting Belief 29
    The Torture of Perfectionism 31
    Are You an Adrenaline Junkie? 33

Chapter 4 MENTAL MASTERY TOOLS 35
    Take Full Responsibility. 35
    What Unique Qualities Do You Bring to
        Your Leadership? 37
    How You Start Your Day, Shapes Your Day 40

Cate Collins

Room Two

Your Emotionally Fit Room

Chapter 5   **FEEL YOUR FEELINGS – FEELINGS ARE NOT FACTS** 45

    Admit Your Feelings. 45
    Feel Your Feelings 47
        Put Pen to Paper 47
        Make an Emotional Debrief Plan 48
    Feeling Safe – At Our Very Cores 49

Chapter 6   **FREEDOM FROM GUILT** 53

    Tripping on Guilt. 53
    Setting Boundaries 54
    Guilt Is a Thing of the Past 55

Chapter 7   **LET GO OF WHAT ISN'T SERVING YOU AND FORGIVE** 57

    What Letting Go Looks Like 58
    Permitting Yourself to Let Go. 60
    Forgiveness Begins with a Decision 61

Chapter 8   **SETTING HEALTHY BOUNDARIES** 65

    Get Honest About Priorities 65
    The Flaw of Perfection 69

Chapter 9   **SURROUND YOURSELF WITH POWERHOUSE PEOPLE** 73

    Your Advisory Table. 73
    Conduct a Relationship Inventory. 75

Chapter 10   **LOVE YOURSELF NOW, NOT WHEN** 79

    Choose Love 79
    The Triple-A Method. 81

Room Three

Your Physically Fit Room

Chapter 11   WHAT IS YOUR BODY TRYING TO TELL YOU?....... 85
- Get to Know Your Body............................ 86
- A Powerhouse Body 86

Chapter 12   HOW ARE YOU SELF-PROTECTING WHILE UNDER STRESS?................................. 89
- The Physical Effects of Stress..................... 89
- Stress Behaviours 91
- Feeding Your Stress 94
- Moving Your Stress 95
- Protecting Your Heart 98
- Your Pain Is a Warning............................ 99
- Mother Nature as a Healer 100

Chapter 13   NOURISHING YOUR BODY WITH HEALTHY FOODS................................. 103
- Listen to Your Body 103
- Body Image 105
- A Powerhouse Eating Plan 107
- The Theory Behind Adrenal Fatigue............... 108

Chapter 14   YOUR HEALTH IS IN THE TOILET 111
- Your Bowel Habits 111
- Helping Your Organs 112
  - Detoxing as a Reset 112
  - Regular Exercise 113
  - Keep Hydrated 113

Chapter 15   SLEEP MATTERS................................. 115
- Are We Experiencing a Sleep Crisis?.............. 115
- Good Sleep Hygiene............................. 117

Cate Collins   ix

Room Four

Your Spiritually Fit Room

Chapter 16	WHAT DOES BEING SPIRITUAL MEAN?	123
	Inner Wisdom and Spirituality	123
	What Does Spirituality Mean to You?	124
Chapter 17	YOUR NEED FOR MEANINGFUL CONNECTION	127
	Loneliness Versus Alone	127
	Connection Is Good for Your Health	128
Chapter 18	HAS YOUR SPIRITUAL GROWTH BECOME STUNTED?	131
	Blocking Your Spirit	131
	A Gratitude Attitude Mindset	133
Chapter 19	THE POSITIVE IMPACT OF MINDFULNESS	137
	The Benefits	137
	Tapping into Your Mindfulness	139
Chapter 20	LET GO, LET JOY IN	143
	Peeling Back the Layers	143
	Finding the Joy	144

Final Thoughts...149
Endnotes..153
Bibliography 157
About the Author...163

Acknowledgements

This book has been a dream for some time and has been birthed with the help of so many amazing, supportive and loving people.

Starting with the obvious, my sweet husband, Victor, who continues to be one of my greatest champions and partners in life. Thank you, sweetheart, for supporting me on so many levels.

To our adult children, Cody and Elisa, for being the beautiful creative spirits that you are and always being a powerful example of resilience, determination and hope. You inspire me more than you know.

Thanks to all my closest friends. Thank you, from the bottom of my heart, for reminding me who I am and to live my purpose. To my brother Mike for our unofficial accountability calls, to my brother Steve and my sister-in-law Marie for sharing their magical retreat and cottage with me so I could write in my earlier days and to my sister Cheryl for being a powerful example of how to be a humble leader. I am grateful to each of you for being there in your own way. To my mom, who has role modelled what resilience, courage, and determination look like, I love you.

My master mind groups continue to be a great source of grounding, wisdom exchange and support. Creating and cheering for each other's success continues to inspire me. Thank you for sharing this journey together. A special shout out to my powerhouse intensive writing group for showing up and reminding each other to "just write." Special thanks to our "Rock star" facilitator Sarah.

To my mentors, Linda and Rosemary, thank you for the countless calls over the times I lost my way or forgot the power of who I was. You continue to hold a very special place in my heart.

To my assistant, Jennifer, who has been a great team player for years and adds great value to my work. I appreciate you very much.

I have huge gratitude to my kind, wise and talented editor, Catherine. Your contribution was key in helping me bring this book to life.

A sincere thank you to all the leaders who kindly endorsed my book. Each of you have touched my life in a very special way.

To the hundreds of powerhouse women who attended my "BE the Leading Lady in Your Own Life" Retreats that continue to go strong. Your willingness to be vulnerable, open and committed to be the best version of yourself touches my soul and urges me to do the same. Thank you.

To my mentor, Jack Canfield, for all your guidance, wisdom, talents, and kindness in making our world a better place.

For all the leaders and teams for trusting me, as they shared their stories, challenges and joy. I continue to learn and grow because of you. Thank you for letting me be your guide. I acknowledge all the leaders who are committed to leading with resilience, courage and confidence by doing their own work and staying true to who they are. We are all in this together and everything is possible. You are making a huge difference. Remember, you are a powerhouse.

Awakening Your Power

"SIT DOWN!" Accompanied by a look that could kill.

Where do I start?

This boss was a piece of work and she was also my greatest teacher – of how *not* to lead.

There were countless times when she created unnecessary drama among our working group, hurled dirty looks during a meeting, chastised team members for requesting help from each other or from her, and neglected appeals for assistance. And to say there was a lack of competent supervision was an understatement. The toll on my body, mind, and spirit was massive, resulting in me suffering a serious burn out.

So why keep working for such a toxic person you might ask? Because this was normal for me, but more about that later.

Part of accepting unacceptable behaviour has elements of denial. One part of you is convinced things will get better and you look into your mental magnifying glass to identify all the great things about your organization and the people in it and, more importantly, the people you serve. After all, my life's purpose is to help people remember the power of who they are.

Did you catch that? *The Powerhouse in You* is about owning your power and connecting with the powerhouse leader in you and yet I was sitting in a cesspool of the polar opposite. Ever find yourself in an ironic situation where the very service you provide to your community is not being delivered among your own staff?

Hence I felt an urgency to write this book for any leader (everyone) who has had their power robbed from them at some point and will benefit from becoming a powerhouse in some area of their life. Today's fast-paced, high intensity, constantly changing, and stressful work environments have gravely impacted your well-being. If you plan to stay in your role or climb the ladder, having a solid plan to help you maintain this tempo together with optimum health and well-being is critical. *The Powerhouse in You* will give you that edge. While other leaders are stressed out and exhausted, on medical leaves, or secretly struggling with their role, you will have an armour of protection by consistently implementing these success habits into your everyday life.

First, I want to validate those past or current areas in your work life where you felt powerless, exhausted, lost, discouraged, trapped, mad as hell at yourself for sticking it out in a toxic work environment, or determined to never let another human being or unhealthy circumstance rent space in your head like that again (especially since they weren't paying rent).

I have had the honour and privilege of working with thousands of leaders and their teams across North America. Self-sabotaging their success was a common theme. My life's work is to help leaders get out of their own way so they will be more joyful, effective and healthier. You can't change what you don't recognize.

Our journey together will allow you to reflect, take inventory, let go of unfinished business with people and situations that once bothered you, give you a new set of glasses to reframe those experiences, and get reacquainted with the power of who you are. As Glinda, the good witch of the north said, "You've always had the power."[1] And finally, to give you simple and powerful tools to consistently *be* that powerhouse leader in all areas of your life.

You may currently be in a toxic relationship at work. The power imbalance may be occurring with your superior, your colleague, your staff, with a community partner. Or you may have come to the other side and are committed to not tolerating this kind of behaviour again and want to learn the tools necessary to prevent a repeat performance. Or perhaps you have not experienced this yet and want to get a jumpstart on your leadership role by avoiding it all together. Possibly your goal is to find effective strategies to help you maintain being a powerhouse leader for the long haul. How well you care for yourself will show up in your leadership delivery. Regardless of the reason you are reading this book, you will experience a positive shift.

If you are looking to stay stuck in blame of the toxic leader or your toxic circumstances, then the ideas we'll be discussing are not for you. *The Powerhouse in You* is about shifting your mindset and shifting responsibility, so you own your power. You deserve better and needn't settle. You are worthy to tell your truth.

My invitation to you is to look for similarities in the stories I share rather than comparing your experiences. The key here is to unite our experiences not further separate us. It's only natural that your ego will want to judge, compare, and stay stuck in the problem, but stay alert and focused on the commonalities and the solutions. The power of one unites us in our stories, experiences, and transformations. You are not alone.

The fact that you are reading this book tells me two things. There is some part of you that is searching for resolution or wanting to add tools to your success tool kit. There may be part of you that questions whether there is hope for change within the organization in which you work. There is. It also tells me you are open to finding another way to do things. When one person changes or shifts in an organization there is a domino effect. Whether your organization is ready for a full-out change remains to be seen. However, you are right where you need to be. Whoever is causing your strife – your boss, your colleague, your employee, your union rep, your board member – they came to you as a teacher. Once you learn the lesson, you get to move on. Whether you stay or whether you leave is a future conversation.

Stay curious. Stay open. Stay willing to think differently and take action. As a powerhouse leader, you will model the healthy behaviours found in these pages. It will make a difference. You will make a difference.

My promise to you is to create a safe space in this journey together, for you to feel accepted, supported, loved, validated, paid witness to, nudged (perhaps even pushed) to take action, and cheering you on every step of the way.

This book is about change. Changing your mindset and changing and recycling your painful experiences to help another person who is going through this. Stay true to yourself by completing the exercises, answering the questions, and especially showing up for yourself to learn, share, and grow. Check my website (https://powerfuljourney.com/thepowerhouseinyou) for free links. Trust yourself to know if the time is not right for you to delve into a particular area. Simply table those exercises for another time. Having supportive and trusting people (such as a therapist, coach, or trusted mentor) around you as you do some of this discovery work is highly recommended.

Expect to be amazed by your "aha" moments. Expect to be amazed by the wave of emotions. Expect to be amazed by your next right steps that you take to be that powerhouse you were always meant to be.

Let's begin your powerful leadership journey.

Chapter 1

What's Power Got to Do with Being a Leader?

Tina Turner's famous song, "What's Love Got to Do with It?" illustrates how her former husband and manager, Ike Turner, took her power away from her. In interviews Tina shared how controlling, vindictive, micromanaging, and possessive and abusive he was during their marriage and her singing career.

But did he take her power away?

In Robert Anthony's book, *Beyond Positive Thinking*, he says "There are no victims, only volunteers."[2] By this, he means that when you tolerate unacceptable behaviour, you volunteer for it.

If I had read this statement during my toxic relationship with my boss, I would have gone ballistic. "How dare you judge me? After all I am a single mother trying to do the best I can." I did not go into the job interview saying I volunteer for whatever you want to dish out to me over the next few years. Having come through the other side, I now understand that once I became aware and could name what was happening then, yes, I did volunteer. I chose to stay working in that toxic environment. This does not mean I deserved it, nor does it mean it was my fault.

Tap into the great wisdom within you. For more powerful exercises and solutions, visit my website: https://powerfuljourney.com/thepowerhouseinyou

A Typical Struggle for Power

An amalgamation is a very common time for power struggles to develop between leaders and their teams. If you or someone you know has experienced a merger, you know that a significant change like this causes different reactions. Some people welcome and roll with change while others respond with different levels of resistance.

In one organization I worked, it became clear to me that incoming team members voiced and called out the dysfunction in our previous system during our agency amalgamation. My previous team was made up of some talented and kind people, however the organization was clearly toxic. There was an attitude of "we will tell you what to think" and "you better stay loyal to this toxic system." Staying loyal included being rewarded for being an informant for the boss. There were clearly defined camps – the supporters, the non-supporters, and the sideline colleagues. Each person did the best they could to adapt.

The supporters were the cheerleaders for the leaders, regardless of how they mistreated certain staff. The non-supporters questioned our leaders when they weren't supporting our team or our service delivery in healthy ways. Finally, the sidelined team members chose not to invest in the drama and were very detached and committed to staying under the radar. Brainstorming ideas seemed to be received as a personal attack versus a healthy exchange of experiences and thoughts. Regardless of the survival role, each one of us gave our power away at different times.

Each organization had their own vision that had some similarities but were very different in some ways too. Clearly team members were grieving their former structure as it showed up in the form of resistance, staying in the past, gossip, waves of emotions that erupted in supervision and team meetings, as well as fear of developing new relationships. How we did business, or in our case how we served our communities, was not "business as usual." We had to come together to reinvent who we were with the intention of serving our communities better.

Can you relate to any of this? As a leader, creating space for your team to grieve during this sort of situation is important. Recognizing and appreciating that some staff may be experiencing stress at home and amalgamation only adds stress to their lives is important. The leaders in my organization sadly missed the boat and personalized comments. The more they pushed to "move on," the more resistance came. I share this experience of what not to do as a leader as mergers and down-sizing are more the norm today due to smaller budgets and reduced funding.

Patrick Lencioni's philosophy and research are helpful here.[3] He highlights that without building a strong foundation, there is no achieving the higher-level goals. Dysfunction occurs when there is:

- an absence of trust,
- fear of conflict,
- lack of commitment,
- avoidance of team accountability, and
- inattention to team objectives.

Accepting Powerlessness

It's important to acknowledge the dark, deceptive, demeaning side of leadership and power as it permeates and destroys organizational relationships and impacts service delivery. That dark side is within each one of us. The part of us that wants to be right, to be acknowledged at all costs, to receive the full credit, to be the winner, to be the star and to know it all. Stay open and willing to do whatever it takes to be the very best leader and human being you can. Part of this will be to own when you are misusing your power.

Becoming the powerhouse leader you are meant to be starts with accepting where in your leadership you are powerless. There are some times that no matter what you do, say, or how you turn yourself into a pretzel, you can't change people, solve their problems, or control their behaviour. There will be times you feel powerless over your own feelings. Accepting this powerlessness will be important for you to learn and grow.

You can influence people, but you don't have the power to change them. Ironically within that powerlessness lies you owning your power. Much like the Serenity Prayer,[4] having awareness of when you are trying to control someone or something or you feel someone or something is trying to control you is important. Accepting to choose what you can control – yourself and your own motives – leads to taking appropriate action. Using this prayer will help you let go, prioritize, and focus on where you have the greatest influence. When you focus on principles versus personalities everyone wins.

When you focus on principles versus personalities everyone wins.

Cate Collins

Think of the number of hours you spend at work with your colleagues. Is it more time than you spend with your family? In my leadership retreats and training, I focus on one important element when it comes to workplace relationships: whatever unfinished business you have with someone in your family of origin, you can expect it to play itself out in your workplace. In my work with leaders and their teams I use the same family system lens I used when I was a family and children's counsellor.

When little "Johnny" was referred to our organization because of his so-called "bad behaviour" (disruptive, not following the rules, etc.), he was simply the barometer in the family. His conduct demonstrated that something wasn't working in the family system. Working with the parents (leaders) consistently shed light on the purpose behind Johnny's actions. Often, I would hear inconsistent rules were being applied, one parent was not being fair at times and showing favouritism, there was lack of a team approach from both parents, and miscommunication was a big challenge. Clearly these parents loved their children, but unless we dug deep enough to get to the source of Johnny's poor behaviour, they would continue to spin their wheels and his performance would get worse. Working with these parents, often uncovered ill-equipped parenting skills, struggles with their own self-esteem, addiction or financial struggles, or experiences of a long history of broken trust, unhealthy relationships, or abuse. How leaders choose to lead sets the tone for an organization.

For me, when I experienced the toxic relationship with my boss, I was also undergoing it with my husband at the time. Like the saying goes, "Wherever I go, there I am." When I look back to all the conflicted relationships I experienced, I was the common denominator. The lesson of accepting unacceptable behaviour kept on repeating itself until I finally woke up and realized I needed to make some changes. I needed to do things differently. I needed to show up differently to get different results. I needed to own my power.

Have You Given Your Power Away?

Jane was a highly successful HR Director of a hospital. She was very proud of the fact that she owned her own home before the age of 50. Her parents never owned their home and although she appreciated that they raised nine children, she was determined she would be a homeowner. The cost of her razor-sharp focus was her marriage.

When Jane first came to me, she felt heart broken, lost, and confused. She could not understand why her husband would just up and leave her. I remember her crossed arms as she declared, "We never even fought." Through Jane's counselling sessions it became clear to her that her extremely long hours at work and taking work home at night left little room for her marriage to grow. She began to understand that healthy arguing or fighting demonstrates that both parties are invested in the marriage. The key is that these exchanges are done with the intention to problem solve, with respect and kindness rather than blame. This is not always easy in the heat of the moment.

In Jane's situation she did not give her power away to her husband. She gave her power away to a limiting belief that told her that being a home-owner meant safety, security, and living a happy life.

Six months following our work together, Jane and her husband reunited, and she brought with her a sincere commitment to keep her priorities in check, namely their relationship being at the top of the list next to her relationship with herself.

I know I have given my power away in a variety of ways. Many of those situations occurred when I was unclear as to who I was. I was much like a chameleon. I became who you wanted me to be so I could get your approval. Some refer to this as people pleasing. Back then my work and helping others defined me. They trumped my needs by miles. Can you relate?

> *At the core of why you give away your power is that you don't love yourself.*

Getting caught up in how I could help my clients, my family, and my friends gave me purpose, and it also made me sick. I suffered a serious burn out some years ago as a result. Whether it was my workplace, my first marriage, my family of origin, or friends, I was a lost soul because I did not connect with the power of who I was. Hence *The Powerhouse in You* was born. My hope is my book will help to show you what not to do or what rabbit hole to avoid going down when it comes to standing in your power.

When you feel helpless, rageful, powerless, or frustrated, you likely are feeling some form of victimization from an event or a person. Feeling victimized is a dangerous place to stay. Acknowledging these feelings is a great start in taking back your power, but the key is not to set up victim camp. "Do you know what he/she did to me? If you knew what I went through you would feel this way too?"

The pitfall with living here is you get to blame, complain, and give your power away to others, not to mention the number of squandered hours of unhappiness. Think of someone who is still nursing an old resentment from years ago and how it has impacted their well-being.

During my presentation, "Is Your Leadership Underwear Too Tight," I ask participants to think of a past emotional wound that still lives on in their memory. I get them to write it down and then rip it out of their books. I proceed to ask, "How many of you have had this hurt or resentment or anger or rage toward this person or event for one month?" Most hands go up.

"How many of you have had this hurt or resentment or anger or rage towards this person or event for six months?" A few hands might come down. We go up to 30 and 40 years. Each time I ask participants to look around the room and notice how many hands remain in the air.

Then I ask, "How has this hurt or resentment or anger or rage towards that person or event seeped into your current relationships?" Common answers include: it erodes their trust, their self-confidence, their peace of mind, their ability to love, and the list goes on. Finally, I ask them, "Are you about done yet giving your power away?" The heads nod "yes."

I ask everyone collectively to rip up the page where they scribed the person's name or the event and say aloud, as they toss their bits of paper into a garbage pail, "I set you free. I set myself free. I am worthy of love and peace. I now own my power." It is an effective symbol of letting go of this hurt or resentment.

What does this letting go exercise have to do with owning your power in the workplace? Whatever is unresolved in your past will resurface in the present. Since we spend all of these hours at work, guess where, usually, it gets triggered? Use Exercise 1 as a great chance to make a list of the people and behaviours you have given your power to.

A great book to help you navigate letting go of any kind is *The Language of Letting Go*.[5] It is a daily meditation book that provides practical and simple tools to let go of unrealistic expectations. It is one of my go-to books.

We will be doing a deep dive into your primary limiting beliefs in Room One, Your Mentally Fit Room.

Exercise 1
WHERE DO YOU GIVE YOUR POWER AWAY?

Warning: If you are in an emotionally fragile place, table this exercise for another time. Having supports around you like a therapist, coach, or a trusted mentor to review what comes up will be important.

This is a personal inventory, much like a business inventory that is a fact-finding and fact-facing process. It is an attempt to discover the truth about what products or, in this case, what behaviours or people are no longer serving you. In the case of the business owner, one objective is to identify damaged or unsalable goods and to get rid of them immediately without regret. In order to be successful, they cannot afford to pretend something is working when it's not. The cost is too high.

By taking an honest view of how you give your power away it allows you to become more aware of how you block yourself from achieving your goals and what matters most. This deeper awareness will help you name, release, and replace this behaviour or how you choose to stand in your power differently with others.

At the top of a page, on the left, write "People." Then in the middle of the page write "Behaviours." The names in your left column are not meant to line up with the unhealthy behaviour you list on the right-hand side of the page. This is an opportunity to do a mind dump, so to speak about who and what you give your power away to. Simply write what first comes to mind. If you catch yourself analyzing it, walk away and revisit it when you are able to stay in flow and without judgement.

By behaviours I mean eating too much sugar, working too many hours and days, obsessive shopping, excessive helping, unwarranted worrying, basically anything that is out of balance and causes you stress.

Be sure to put your name at the top of your list. By putting your name at the top of the list, you are acknowledging that you give your power away to your thinking and limiting beliefs and there is work to be done in correcting this.

Here are a few to help get you started.

People	Behaviours
Me	overindulging on sugar, chips, alcohol, caffeine
my parent(s)	comparing/competing success, body image
sibling(s)	excessive shopping, sleeping, TV
boss/co-worker	gossiping

past/current relationship   constant worrying, self-doubting, perfectionism, people pleasing, helping others too much
spouse/child/friend   feel "not good, smart, or worthy enough"

If you were to take just 10% more responsibility for your health, your peace of mind, and your life, which person or behaviour needs your attention right now? Circle the one thing that will have the greatest impact in other areas of your life.

Now I would like you to write this sentence at the top of another page, leaving lots of room for writing.

"I give my power away to _____ (fill in what you circled) because _____."

It will look like this on the page.

I give my power away to <u>my boss or superior (Executive Director, CEO, or board of directors)</u> because <u>I want her approval, recognition, to feel special, important, safe, or supported.</u>

I give my power away to <u>my boss</u> because …

Keep writing this sentence over and over again and let the answers pour on to the page until you feel you have fully answered the question. This will be healthy venting. Once you have filled the page(s) sit back and look for the main theme.

Let's explore that first example.

I give my power away to <u>my boss</u> because <u>I want her approval, recognition, to feel special, important, safe, or supported.</u>

As long as you are feverishly trying to get her attention, whose attention are you ignoring? Exactly. The attention from yourself. Once you are fulfilling all of these qualities for yourself, it will be less important for you to hopelessly chase after someone else's approval. The approval that is most important is from yourself, especially if your boss is detached or is unkind to you. Remember they lack self-love for themselves. They can't give it to you because they don't have it themselves. Do you deserve a boss who will show up for you, who will have your back, who will mentor and support you along your journey? Absolutely!

You've heard the phrase, "When people show you who they are, believe them." The reality is that your boss's actions have proven this likely won't happen today and it's time to surrender to the idea that they likely won't be able to. However, once you move your attention from your boss to you, freedom follows. You will stop chasing something that may never happen.

Have You Robbed Someone of Their Power?

Stealing someone's power happens directly, bluntly, and subtly. Direct is fairly obvious. You discourage staff from asking questions or critique their comments. You use jokes or flippant remarks that are passive-aggressive to make them feel small or less, primarily so that you can elevate your ego. You remind them regularly how lucky they are to have a job. You use condescending or intimidating behaviour.

> *Stealing someone's power happens directly, bluntly, and subtly.*

Blunt methods of robbing a staff member of their power include yelling or cursing, or both, at them in front of other employees. This of course is abusive. You wouldn't accept someone talking to your daughter, son, or parent this way.

More subtle ways of robbing someone of their power is to micromanage your employees by checking up on their progress at every step or hovering over their work. You may neglect or do last minute employee reviews, giving them the message that their performance and contributions to the organization are not valued. You talk about other team members in negative ways or gossip with one or more staff. You don't include staff in related work meetings, notifying them that you will tell them later rather than giving them an opportunity to attend. When you scold or criticize one of your team members during a staff or team meeting, you have robbed them not only of their power but respect and dignity too. Toxic environments reflect badly on you as their leader.

Whether you turn a blind eye to what is really going on or you actively participate, you are responsible for shifting your culture. I know it can get discouraging if you have inherited a toxic team culture. Your determination to help shift it by hiring outside consultants, trainers, or leadership coaches will pay dividends. Your actions will not go unnoticed by your organization. Change takes time, but it is worth it. You may need to open your eyes and your heart to the possibility that there may be times when you are not showing up with the best version of yourself. When you are deprived of sleep, have unhealthy eating habits, overcommit yourself, doing the job of three people instead of one, you are bound to make mistakes. You can't change what you don't recognize. If you are unhappy chances are so is your team.

I worked with a manager who repeatedly said, "My staff are entitled whiners who don't even show up and do their job right." If she was telling a stranger that, I can only imagine how those thoughts manifested into her behaviour. Don't get me wrong. There will be times when you think negatively about your staff. If, however, this is your constant thought process, this is a red flag that something needs to be changed.

When a leader demonstrates authenticity, trust, respect, integrity, consistency, competency, and an openness to do the very best they can, their employees want to show up the best way they can. Have their backs and they will have your back. They want to be engaged, be focused on the solution, be a team player, and deliver the best service possible. You set the tone for your culture. The opposite is also true. If a leader is defensive, closed, critical, has unrealistic expectations of others, has anger outbursts, gossips about team members, manipulates, or talks down to their team, they can expect an increased turnover rate, minimal engagement, high sick leave, more conflict, and extreme stress among employees. Pay attention to the feedback in your organization. Look for the red flags well before your organization is in crisis.

You rob others of their power when you ignore the elephant in the room. Anonymous surveys, regular authentic conversations at team meetings and during supervision, and suggestion boxes are just some of the ways to gather the pulse of what your team members are really thinking. Ask them on a scale from 1 to 10, with 10 being high and 1 being low, where would you rate me as your supervisor? What would I need to do to bring that number higher? Having courageous conversations opens the door to greater trust and loyalty. When employees can share the truth of how they feel without paying for it later, it allows the team to unite and collaborate more effectively. Keep in mind, much like a family, your team will have times when it seems everyone is on the same page and working collaboratively and other times conflict and disengagement will be present. As their leader, they need you to step up and acknowledge the elephant and be willing and open to brainstorming how to get the team back on track. Regular staff retreats and training that includes communication, conflict resolution, and trust building will help.

As I shared before whatever unfinished business you have with siblings or your parents gets played out in your workplace. So that enmeshed relationship with your brother or sister will be recreated at work. That aggressive relationship with a sibling will too. That disconnected "we all live on islands" dynamic is the lens through which you relate to others.

Think of a strained or unhealthy relationship you have at work. Who do they remind you of from your childhood or your family? Although this person may be a different age, gender, or culture, similar feelings get triggered and old patterns of behaviour are resurrected.

I worked with two managers who were stuck in an intense conflict with each other and each felt the other was robbing them of their power. It was affecting their performance and their teams felt they needed to take sides. Gossip was rampant. Team engagement suffered because others were being triggered by the open disregard and lack of respect the managers showed for each other. These two intelligent, seasoned, and talented managers were turning into closed-minded, over-reactive, and unhappy people. They both needed a time out.

When I met individually with them to have them share what was going on for them, it quickly became clear that each of them was triggering the other from past relationships. During each of their one-on-one sessions I asked, "Where have you felt this kind of intensity before?" One manager replied, "My brother. He always dismissed my point of view. He thought he was superior to me. He was a jackass to me!" The other manager shared that her colleague reminded her of her mother. Her mother rarely gave her compliments. She critiqued everything she did. If she brought a paper home with a B, she asked why it wasn't an A? She shared how she never felt good enough for her approval. Clearly the two of them were operating from old scripts from their past and were being triggered.

Fortunately, each manager was willing and committed to delve in and make peace with their past relationship. Their new-found awareness, coupled with addressing their unfinished business from past relationships, allowed them to ask themselves two important questions.

1. Does my reaction fit the current circumstances or am I reacting from the past?
2. How can I make the situation better?

They each came out the other side able to see how the other was simply a teacher to help them address this unfinished business. Since both felt heard, paid witness to, and supported during our one-on-one coaching sessions, they were able to shift their focus on how they contributed to the conflict. The two came together for a session and the tension had subsided. Each was able to express their desire to build their relationship and show up better than they had with specific behaviour changes. By the end of the session, the two embraced. These managers went on to be each other's allies for many years. By cleaning up their side of the street, it freed them up to enjoy and even admire each other's leadership strengths.

Not all workplace conflicts where you take responsibility for your part of robbing someone's power ends this way. The important thing is you remain honest when you make a mistake, when you rob someone of their power, and you sincerely correct it as soon as you can. Because you *will* rob someone of their power. We all do. Do the right thing no matter what the circumstance is. Remain open to how you feel following an interaction. If you feel unsettled or feel bad about yourself, likely your ego got involved and took over. Stay willing to learn and grow from these experiences. It is when you stay in denial and dismiss the verbal, physical, or written feedback from your staff or your superior that you are destined for trouble. If your thought process is, "If only they listened to me and did it this way, we wouldn't be in this mess," please pay close attention. You are stuck in blame.

It takes two to be in a relationship. How this plays out is within your control. I have seen some leaders stay stuck in resistance and refuse to see their part in a conflict. The stress spills out in all facets of their life. They experience constant headaches or stomach aches, put on extra weight or they lose weight, they become depressed, constantly second guess themselves, become paranoid, fixated on black and white thinking versus collaborative thinking, obsess about the problem, take out their frustration on their spouse or children or they may withdraw and isolate. There is a price to pay when we are inflexible in our thinking and are committed to being the innocent party or the victim.

Chapter 2

What Does It Mean to Be a Powerhouse?

Think of a leader in your life who inspires you. What qualities do you admire most?

- Is it their confidence?
- Do they set healthy boundaries?
- Do they seem aligned with their purpose at all times?
- Are they great communicators?
- Do they appear comfortable with conflict?
- Do they get things done effectively?

Would you agree, they likely have successful habits that support them?

My colleague and friend, Nancy, is a great example of someone owning their power. I remember one day sliding into her office, much like Kramer from the sitcom *Seinfeld* (minus the hair – well, most days) to ask for her help with a complicated family I was working with. With one finger in the air, and her eyes glued to her computer, she said she needed to finish her report for a court case she was involved in and was due now. "Cate, I'm all yours at noon, however it is really important for me to get this done." With my head hung low I sauntered back to my office disappointed I did not have the opportunity to brainstorm with my colleague about my client.

Tap into the great wisdom within you. For more powerful exercises and solutions, visit my website: https://powerfuljourney.com/thepowerhouseinyou

Then I realized, she wasn't saying Cate you are unimportant to me. She was saying what I am doing is equally important and it needs my attention first. Do you see the gift she gave me?

When someone comes from their place of power it allows more trust, more collaboration, more respect, more kindness, and, yes, love. I felt closer to Nancy when she was truthful with me as opposed to staying in my own narrative of rejection and hurt. By setting this healthy boundary, she role modelled the importance of owning your power.

Finding Your Powerhouse Qualities

Being a powerhouse leader means gaining clarity on who you are and what you uniquely bring to the leadership table. Once you know it, it's easy to own it. Having a leadership vision statement will be an effective strategy to keep you grounded and purposeful in your role. I have included a powerful vision statement exercise in Room One, Your Mentally Fit Room (see Exercise 2). Feel free to go there now to help you be crystal clear as to what makes you distinctly you as a powerhouse leader. This vision statement will act as a lighthouse during stressful times and keep you centered in your values, strengths, skills, and talents. The more you know who you are, the clearer and more intentional you will be in owning your power.

> *Being a powerhouse leader means gaining clarity on who you are and what you uniquely bring to the leadership table.*

Keep in mind during this journey that you are a human and will make mistakes. Accept your imperfections. These errors do not make you a bad person. Bring that humanness to your leadership role. Regardless of your age, there are still parts of you that are still growing up and into the person you are meant to be. How you shift your perspective from blame is to sincerely look at your part in any relationship.

Stay curious. Stay open. Stay willing to do whatever it takes to work this through. You either deal with it now or you should expect a similar experience to occur in the future. This will not go away.

The benefits are great when you own your power. Here are some of them.

- Take full responsibility for all your choices.
- Remove yourself as a victim from past or current situations by owning your part.
- Awareness of how to interrupt your self-sabotage patterns of reverting to old, unhealthy coping behaviours (e.g., co-dependency behaviour, or neglecting exercise and eating healthier) and replace them with healthy choices.
- Knowing how to set clear boundaries and when your boundaries are being violated.
- Awareness when you are jumping into rescue mode to avoid looking at what you need and want, and course correct.
- You speak your truth with clarity, love, and assertion.
- By aligning with your purpose as a powerhouse leader.

The transition won't happen overnight, and it will not be easy. It will involve some reflection and possibly looking at some parts of yourself you don't want to see. A plan can help, a blueprint, if you will. You can't build a powerhouse without a plan and my four Rooms will help you explore the various aspects and keep you focussed.

Your Powerhouse and the Four Rooms

Some years back I created a success framework that has been a game changer for leaders and teams that I have worked with across North America. I use this framework in my presentations, my retreats, and my coaching internationally. It's quite simple, but it evolved over time.

Several years ago, I had just moved to a new area and felt out of place and unsure of how I was going to build my training company. Following a meditation group I joined, I shared my concerns with a wise Indigenous man who shared something very practical and profound.

He said, "Cate, in our tribe we believe that in order for us to remain grounded, focused, live in our purpose and especially own our power, we must enter each of these Four Rooms every day. These Four Rooms include your Mental Room, your Emotional Room, your Physical Room and your Spiritual Room. Each of us are responsible for entering each of our Four Rooms daily. Much like a house where some rooms are empty and other rooms are packed with things, our Four Rooms need balance. We need balance in order to show up as the best person we can be."

I liked the metaphor of the Four Rooms, so I tweaked and developed his Four Rooms further. Eventually I adapted some of my Pilates training to include the idea of the powerhouse.

As a certified Pilates instructor, I repeatedly say to fitness members, "Engage your core" because everything comes from your core. Most people think that your core is solely your outer abdominal muscles, but you can have a six-pack and still have weak core muscles. Much like owning your power that comes from deep within you, the same is true for your core or your powerhouse. My members embraced the term "powerhouse" and I encouraged them to think, feel, and act as if they already were a "powerhouse" not only in their body's but their minds, emotions, and their spirit.

This idea morphed into my leadership training. A common theme among the successful leaders I worked with was they forgot to connect with the power within themselves in some area of their life, which caused them unnecessary pain. Engaging their power as a leader meant entering each of these Four Rooms daily. I added "fit" to each Room because entering your Mental Room didn't mean you were experiencing healthy thoughts. The term "fit" symbolized the end goal of wanting to have balance and peace of mind in that Room. When you are mentally fit and engaging in activities that calm and quiet your mind, it allows you to be more focused and effective.

Each of the Rooms are interconnected with each other. Let's say you are very disciplined with planning and preparing your schedule to meet your goals. You may enter your Mentally Fit Room regularly by meditating or creating quiet time to do that planning. (Congratulations! This is a fabulous habit.) However, if that planning doesn't include entering into your Emotionally Fit Room to connect with supportive people in your life or you neglect to take health breaks to nourish your body and mind with healthy food and relaxation, it will take a toll on your Spiritually Fit Room by robbing you of your joy and happiness. Each of these Four Rooms can handle a little neglect for short periods, much like the dust colleting in the corner of your guest room at home, however if the avoidance and inattention is severe, if the ants build a colony, you are in trouble.

Keeping these Four Rooms top of mind and checking in and taking action daily will act as a lighthouse during your leadership journey and your life so you will be more mindful, more confident, effective, and more joyful.

*Check in with your Mentally Fit Room first.
Everything starts with a thought, impacting
your Emotionally Fit Room then into your
Physically and Spiritually Fit Rooms.*

There is a reason you check in with your Mentally Fit Room first. Everything starts with a thought, impacting your Emotionally Fit Room then into your Physically Fit Room and finally your Spiritually Fit Room. As you check into each of these Rooms, think of how you might thoroughly clean a room in your home. Likely, you would pick up and examine each item to see if it still fits or is useful to you today. Some things you might dust off or polish them up and go back to using them. Other things you will need to repair or fix in order to serve their purpose. And other things will not serve you any longer and need to be let go.

Once your room is thoroughly clean, don't you feel happier or more content? The same is true when you spend time in one of the Four Rooms of your powerhouse. As you check or plug in you are recharged – you've powered your house. Spending time in a Room also allows for ideas and solutions to surface. The more you remain open and willing to experiment with new things for that particular Room, namely my success habits, the more effective, joyful, and healthy you will be. When you spend too much time in any one Room your powerhouse becomes imbalanced and it's easier for you to fall off the leadership beam.

Becoming a Powerhouse

You have all the power you need right now within you from your Higher Power, Universe, God, Nature.[6] All of the power of divine love, intelligence, and wisdom is available to you. It is your fear that blocks you from fully stepping into your power. Staying busy distracts you from feeling this fear and doing the necessary reality check to overcome it and focus on what needs your attention in some area of your life.

I love an exchange in the movie, *The Holiday*,[7] where two women swap houses due to boyfriend issues. There is a scene where Kate Winslet (Iris) is with Eli Wallach (Arthur) in a restaurant and Arthur says, "You, I can tell are a leading lady but for some reason you are acting like the best friend." Iris replies, "You're so right. You are supposed to be the leading lady in your own life for God's sake."

You deserve this for yourself in whatever area of your life you are not owning your power. The only way to connect with the powerhouse within you is to step in the sticky stuff along the way that reeks of old hurts, resentments, and limiting beliefs that keep you stuck and repeating the same old results. You deserve better.

Coming from a place where you can serve enhances you on your powerful leadership journey. When you check in and take action in each of your Four Rooms regularly – your Mentally, Emotionally, Physically, and Spiritually Fit Rooms – owning your power will be effortless.

Let's have some fun as we explore my Four Rooms success blueprint for optimum health and performance.

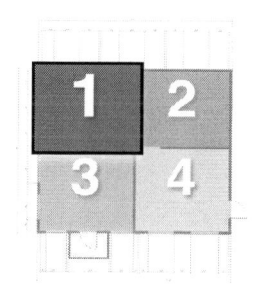

Room One

YOUR MENTALLY FIT ROOM

Begin by entering your Mentally Fit Room. Let's imagine you are wearing a monitoring device that allows a team of researchers to monitor your thoughts throughout your day. What will they find? I know, a scary thought, right?

The truth is it's easy to find successful leaders, but hard to find mentally fit ones. The stresses and perks of your leadership role position take their mental toll on you, as well as emotional, physical, and spiritual stresses. Others define you by your leadership role and it's easy to become disconnected to who you truly are inside that role. After all, so many depend on you at work and home.

Just ask anyone close to you – family member, colleague, or your assistant – if they notice any changes in you when you are staying in your head too long. Their answer will likely be that you are more disconnected, forgetful, impatient, and frustrated. One leader shared, "Being in my head too long can be the most dangerous neighbourhood I have ever walked in, and I try not to stay in it too long because eventually bad things happen."

In this Room, we will seek out the mental blind spots that can deter you in your leadership followed by mental mastery tools. Sometimes one pattern of negative thinking can lead to another and it's essential to identify the source for each so that you can counteract its influence.

Let's check in to your Mentally Fit Room.

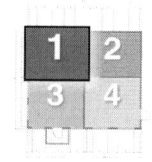

Chapter 3

Mental Blind Spots

I am referring to your blind spot much like the blind spot you have when driving your car. When your attention is focused straight ahead only and you forget to turn your head to check your side mirrors, you can potentially cause or get into a car accident. As a leader you have a certain way of thinking and doing things. If you become inflexible or unwilling to discard old ways of thinking or unhealthy leadership habits you run the risk of causing damage to your organization through disengaged teams, miscommunication, hampering success, and ineffective service delivery.

As we go through each mental blind spot see if you have experienced any of these traps and highlight which areas you want to improve or change.

Distorted Belief System

Becky was known in many organizations as a "well-respected and competent leader" because of her high performance and engaged team, serving on many committees, being the right arm to her boss, and for being all-around likeable. Her husband was dashingly handsome, and they had two boys together who she adored. There was one catch: she was cheating on her husband.

We all have areas in our lives that we aren't particularly proud of. Secrets keep us sick. The weight of Becky's secret was weighing heavy on her. Becky and I met when I was facilitating a seminar called "When

---

Tap into the great wisdom within you. For more powerful exercises and solutions for your Mentally Fit Room, visit my website: https://powerfuljourney.com/mentallyfitroom

to Stay, When to Leave." Some participants came because they wanted to leave their jobs and others, like Becky, came because they struggled with whether to leave their marriage. She found it so helpful that she wanted to work with me one on one as an executive coaching client to discuss her dilemma further.

As our sessions began, I sensed there was a link between Becky cheating on her husband and her connection with her father, but she kept avoiding the topic. Finally, I asked her to humour me and let me get a better understanding of her relationship with her father.

Becky shifted uncomfortably in her chair and rubbed her arm. "I was ten, but I remember like it was yesterday," she said gazing at the floor. "I was in the kitchen late one night getting a glass of water and I overheard my mom and dad yelling at each other from their bedroom. I couldn't hear all of it, but I could hear my mom crying really loud. I did hear her say, 'Why? Why Dave do you keep doing this to us? Am I not good enough for you? Is she pretty? Is she younger? What about the kids? What do I tell them?' Come to think of it, my dad kept yelling over and over, 'I'm done with all of this. I've had it.' The next morning when I woke up my dad was gone, vanished. We never saw him again. My mom was a wreck. I just took over. I cooked. I cleaned the house. I did my homework. I even looked after my little brother. I was convinced if I did everything right, my dad would come back home."

The room was silent for a long moment. Then Becky sobbed like a child for the father she loved so dearly. If only she had cleaned up her mess after school, her father would have come back home – or so she thought.

The truth behind any problem or issue is the story you tell yourself to make sense of it all. This is where you become your own worst enemy – if your "thinking" is misguided.

Fear-Based Narratives

You've heard the phrase, "It's all in your head." Think of a time when you might respond with fear. The event could be an injury or illness that you or a loved one is experiencing, the threat of your job terminating, or a challenge in your relationship. Immediately, your mind begins to tell you the story connected to that event. It shows you the negative image of what might happen. The voice in your head is concerned about what you may lose or how you will be forced to change – you may have to sell the house, or he is clearly leaving you. Fear grabs you by the throat and your fight or flight response is activated. Now both your body and mind are flooded with the feeling of fear. As this fear mounts, you feel inadequate to deal with the event and worry takes over with the "what ifs."

You don't want to feel any kind of suffering and you avoid it at all costs.

This is normal wiring. Your mind protects itself from the very image it created. And so, the cycle continues. An event occurs, your mind creates a negative image, fear jumps up to guide you, and you have a train wreck. Guy Finley shares a brilliant quote that simplifies this process.[8] "When it comes to fear, the fear is real, but the why is a lie." He uses the example of a child crying out to his parent because of the monsters in his bedroom. The parent assures her child that, yes, she understands that he feels real fear, but it was a shadow he saw, and there are no monsters.

Your mind convinces you the event is much bigger than you and that it has power and control over you. The truth is that you are much bigger than the event or the image that your mind has created.

Fear plays tricks on you by feeding you sabotaging thoughts so that you become immobilized. Some call it "analysis paralysis." You may lose sleep and appetite, and eventually your drive to take action can become so far away that you do nothing. Feeling the fear and mobilizing anyway are the key action steps.

What do you say to your fear? Do you say, "I did blow it last time, and it might happen again if I'm not prepared." Or do you listen to your worries and begin to feed the story it is telling you

The more you train your mind to respond differently, the better the outcome. Let's use the example. In reaction to a colleague's advancement, your mind might tell you this story, "She has been promoted more times than me; they clearly respect her more than me." Now let's take a closer look.

What steps did she take to get that position? Become curious and step away from your ego and pride. "I plan to observe how she interacts with our superiors to see what I can improve on for my next advancement. Maybe I will meet with her for coffee and get to know her better."

Do you see the difference in the thinking? In the first example your fear clearly is in charge and feeding you a fear-based story that may or may not be true. In the second example your thinking comes from a curious, detached, and solution-focused place. Ask yourself, "Is the way I'm thinking the solution or the problem?" This will help you get closer to taking that necessary action.

Remember Becky from the previous section? She had convinced herself that she caused her father to cheat and eventually leave her family home. Her inner voice or critic said when you take care of everyone else's needs, they won't leave you. And they certainly won't betray you.

As a result, she took on the role in her marriage to keep everyone happy and perfect and in check. Deep down she was trying to make up for something that, ultimately, she wasn't responsible for. Rather than talk to her husband about her unhappiness in their marriage, she chose to protect him by saying nothing. Eventually she got tired of stuffing down how she felt about her own needs.

We all think like Becky at different points in our lives. It's natural. But letting fear run our mental narrative is harmful, and it is a mental blind spot most of us must be vigilant to overcome.

> *Letting fear run our mental narrative is harmful. It's a mental blind spot most of us must be vigilant to overcome.*

What is your fear-based narrative? What drives you to work so hard, be the best, deliver high quality leadership? Discovering what this is will help you avoid, not only your blind spots but, unnecessary pain.

Here is a simple and effective technique to master. The next time your fear or negative self-talk shows up, ask it these questions.

- What is it you want me to know?
- How do you want me to fix this?

Think of a time when you were Netflix or TV binging and eating your favourite junk food. What messages did your fear or the voice in your head give you?

For some, it may go something like this. "You are a lazy fat pig. Here you go again pigging out and sitting here like a slob." Perhaps your negative self-talk isn't so hostile, but you get the idea. The result is you feel bad about yourself, have regrets, or maybe wished you watched less TV or ate less junk food. Self-loathing or feeling bad about yourself may carry into a sleepless night, upset stomach, headache, feeling anxious, or any number of things. Believe it or not, but that inner voice is actually your biggest fan.

The important work is to guide your internal voice to reframe how it says things so you can hear it better and reduce the emotional hit.

Back to you sitting around eating junk food and TV binging. When your negative self-talk voices its concerns, it will be important to teach it a better way to communicate these concerns. Tell the voice in your head, "I know you are worried for me right now. What is it you want me to know? It is more helpful when you are kinder to me when you point something out. Let's try this again." Your fear might respond with, "I'm worried if you keep watching all this TV and eating junk you will put your heart at risk and have a heart attack like your father." Next, ask yourself, "How do you want me to fix this?" And your inner voice might say, "I want you to take a walk before or after dinner to release all the stress from your day or get that gym membership you keep talking about."

These two simple questions of, "What is it you want me to know" and "How do you want me to fix this" cut through everything and focuses on the solution versus the emotional badgering.

Your Limiting Belief

Do any of these statements sound familiar?

- Don't get too sure of yourself; the other shoe will drop soon.
- Be careful. They'll find out you're a fraud.
- I am not good enough because my mother was too busy to spend time with me.
- I don't have a clue what I'm doing here.
- If I get close to someone, they will eventually leave me.
- I don't feel worthy of all of this.
- I don't belong here.

Over the years, I've found a theme common with my clients. Regardless of how successful they are, how wonderful their families are, how many raving fans they have for their work, or how many letters they have behind their names, deep inside of them lies a voice of doubt. They feel like frauds or imposters.[9]

I was 40, fairly successful, and knee deep in therapy when I came face to face with my primary limiting belief. I carried this gnawing feeling around that I wasn't worthy enough. Subconsciously, it was a story I told myself many times that kept me separate and alone. Not feeling worthy became the tainted filter system I used in some of my interactions, both in my work and personal life. The collateral damage was great.

There were times I accepted unacceptable behaviour, second guessed myself, questioned why I ended up on the invitation list for special projects or parties, came up short when I compared my accomplishments with my peers, and the list went on. When I would share with a colleague or close friend my fear of failure or not being deserving enough to sit at the success table, they were consistently surprised, since they saw me as very competent.

Through the discovery process of my childhood during therapy, things became crystal clear. My mom had two toddlers at home, was three months pregnant with me, and her doting father suddenly died of a brain aneurysm. She was an only child. Into her final trimester with me, her friend across the hall in their apartment building gave birth to a dead baby. My mom was the source of support and guidance to her grieving mother and her grieving friend all within that nine-month pregnancy.

As I put the pieces of the puzzle together, I was dumbfounded. I had authored two CDs that dealt with loss and grieving, but little did I know it was all connected. I carried my mother's unresolved grief. How do you celebrate life when death is all around you? Having this awareness armed me with new information to transform my limiting belief. You can too.

When I was fortunate to be hand-picked to train with Jack Canfield,[10] he shared that there are three dominant beliefs that each of us possess: I'm not good enough, I'm not worthy enough or I'm not smart enough. Typically, each of us has one primary belief that we operate from. For me, my primary belief was I'm not worthy enough.

What limiting belief keeps showing up for you in your life? Are you struggling with a particular relationship? What challenging work relationships keep occurring? Do you keep losing your cool? Do people tell you that you expect too much from them or from yourself? The constant drive is what got you to where you are; however, it is also what disconnects you from yourself, others, and your higher power, if you don't keep it in check. What self-doubt keeps showing up for you? As they say, "What keeps you up at night?"

The National Science Foundation published an article in 2005, summarizing research on human thoughts per day. It was found that the average person has about 12,000 to 60,000 thoughts per day. Of those thoughts, 80% were negative and 95% were exactly the same repetitive thoughts from the previous day. Yikes!

Imagine for a moment repeating the thought, "I am good enough. I am a powerhouse. I am loving and accepting myself," throughout your day. Is it fair to say that your heart would radiate love and that you would stand in your power with confidence and clarity?

How you view yourself is mirrored in all your relationships, or as Oprah says, "You do not become what you want, you become what you believe."

The Torture of Perfectionism

Betty attended one of my "Be the Leading Lady in Your Own Life" women's retreats. She was humble, confident, quiet, and had travelled several hours to be there. It wasn't until we did a letting go exercise that Betty became very emotional. During this releasing exercise you are to write a letter to yourself for giving your power away to someone or something.

She wrote about the day when she visited her mother to share the exciting news that she had received her PhD. She had worked hard at her studies while employed in a full-time management role. Her mother's response was, "Your cousin is a doctor. This doesn't make you a doctor, right?" Betty was crushed. In her letter she wrote about all the times her mother had discounted her grades when she came home from elementary and high school. If she got an A, her mom wanted to know why it wasn't an A+.

She poured out on paper how the little girl inside of her mourned for the kind of mother who would love and accept and celebrate her. She mourned for how she rented space for her mother in her head even as an adult. She recounted all the times she pushed herself to be perfect at all costs only to have her mother discount her successes. Her constant struggle for approval with her mother permeated into many of her relationships hoping they would give her approval. Of course, she chose friends and partners much like her mother. The cycle continued – until now.

Betty cried deeply for that little girl and young woman who felt invisible. Once she burned the letter, along with the rest of the group, you could see a wave of peace pour over her. She set herself free. Betty took full responsibility for all her choices in that moment. She also uncovered the truth about perfectionism and the source of it. Perfectionism is an illusion that eventually *hurts* you more than it *helps* you. Many type A personality people struggle with this. Our workplace culture rewards perfectionism and the need to be busy all the time.

If only I work harder, faster, smarter on this project, relationship, or situation it will be perfect. Think of the times you got your knickers in such a knot to write that perfect report, say the perfect thing at a staff meeting, or give a perfect presentation. Did you ever ask yourself, "Why did I jump through so many hoops unnecessarily? Who am I trying to be perfect for? Perfectionism is like a gremlin that whispers in your ear, "Not quite perfect yet. It needs more of this or more of that." Meanwhile what you have done is ready to go. Perfect is good. Done is better.

Perfectionism comes about due to low self-esteem, not high self-esteem. Someone with high self-esteem doesn't attach the success of the outcome to their worth. They give the task at hand their best in that moment and refrain from torturing themselves with perfectionism. They prioritize what is most important and focus their energy there as opposed to doing cartwheels for every deadline. They conserve their energy for the most important things rather than continuously burning the candle at both ends.

Strive for excellence absolutely, but perfectionism is a whole other kettle of fish. You know when you are in the perfectionist zone when you are in a repeated state of anxiousness or guilt and have an intense need to do only the best. Often when we are in a perfectionist state, we project this idea out to others and expect the same from them. It is equally destructive as it interferes with their growth and makes them feel ashamed of not measuring up to your standards.

The pressure to do more, be more, and deliver more is real. Get your numbers up, create more innovative programs, do more with less, and the list goes on. You cross off one item only to add three more to your "to do list." Multitasking – working on a proposal, staff walking in with a question, and dings from your technology – contributes to brain fog. Many leaders struggle with jumping from one activity to another and often lose focus. These constant distractions put your body, mind, and spirit into a state of feeling overwhelmed. And we wonder why our minds struggle with winding down at night. I will explore more about staying in flow in your Spiritually Fit Room, but you will find the following strategies very helpful.

From his 2009 study,[11] researcher Clifford Nass was able to offer up two helpful tactics.

1. Limit the number of things you juggle at any given time to just two tasks.
2. Use the "20-minute rule." Instead of constantly switching between tasks, try to fully devote your attention to one task for 20 minutes before switching to the other.[12]

Successful leaders know that expecting responsible behaviour from yourself is important, however keeping perfectionism in check will allow you to lighten up and enjoy the journey.

Are You an Adrenaline Junkie?

A close cousin of perfectionism is the rush you receive from putting out fires. Adrenaline increases your heart rate, elevates your blood pressure, and boosts energy supplies. Cortisol, the primary stress hormone, increases sugars (glucose) in the bloodstream, enhances your brain's use of glucose, and increases the availability of substances that repair tissues.

Look around in your organization for people who thrive on the adrenaline rush that comes with jumping into the "fight" response to tackle a problem or de-escalate a situation. Typically, we think of police officers, fire fighters, or the military when it comes to serious hits of adrenaline. If you have been in your role for some time no doubt you have observed major changes with the pace, the intensity, and the constant stress you and your team endure. Your body, mind, and spirit can only endure so much of the fight response before it burns out. Each person has varying degrees of stress overload and parachuting in a physical vacation for one to two weeks per year is not enough to deal with it.

When you look at the times you took your power back by making a better decision to not live in that excess drama and crisis, things shifted. Your awareness gave you permission to make different choices. I bet some of the choices were uncomfortable. Likely you had to detach from an unhealthy relationship, step off a committee, stand up to a boss, take an early vacation, or you shifted your focus and decided not to be the cavalry riding in to save the day or the person in crisis. Changing the lens of how you need to show up is a meaningful way to take your power back.

Regular check-ins with yourself are important. Tragically, when your primary focus is on "putting out fires" all the time, long work hours, taking work home, and having no clear boundary between work and home, danger awaits you. We will explore in more detail how your body supports you by cuing you with signs to slow down, pause, or take a break in your Physically Fit Room. If you identify as someone who thrives under pressure and enjoys the rush of the crisis, having this awareness is a great start.

Finding ways to manage it will be revealed in these pages.

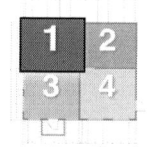

Chapter 4

Mental Mastery Tools

Now that you have identified your mental blind spots, it's time to address them in more effective and helpful ways.

For your mental mastery tools, I want to concentrate on solution-focused decisions you can make to work through fear, change, and discord. The three mental mastery tools I provide are meant to simplify and bring clarity and power to your decisiveness.

Take Full Responsibility

Mary had worked in a very toxic organization where fear and scarcity thinking was like a fast-growing cancer. Thirty per cent of the staff had either quit or gone on sick leave due to the dysfunctional work environment. "Everyone was busy walking on eggshells around the CEO because of her autocratic and undermining leadership style. She suffocated our creativity, team engagement, and our passion to show up in our own best management style. It was exhausting! I spent most of my time putting out emotional fires with my team due to the CEO's overreactions."

Mary agreed she had given way too much power away to her CEO for too long. It was clear to her that she was not valued or acknowledged for her leadership contributions. The more Mary tried to address the power struggle, the more she was greeted with resistance, blame, and shame. Her loyalty to her organization and her team was evident. Her

---

Tap into the great wisdom within you. For more powerful exercises and solutions for your Mentally Fit Room, visit my website: https://powerfuljourney.com/mentallyfitroom

health and well-being were at stake. Her preoccupation with work kept her up at night, she gained 15 pounds, was frequently unavailable to her family due to exhaustion and taking work home, and her quality of life had diminished considerably. She had lost her joy and passion. After yet another sleepless night, Mary woke up to the realization that enough was enough. She took her power back. She began looking for work elsewhere and was fortunate to land an even better job.

In order to connect with the powerhouse leader in you, it all starts with taking full responsibility for your choices. The power in that statement lies in *you* owning your power – not a situation. Not another person. Not your organization. Not the government. Not your employee. Not your spouse. There are times when this is a hard pill to swallow, especially when someone has tried to control, manipulate, intimidate, abuse, dismiss, or harm you in some way. When you make a decision to stop complaining, stop blaming others, stop minimizing your part in the situation, or justifying your actions, you free up your energy to stand up for what matters to you and to own your power.

There is nothing attractive or sexy about being a martyr, a whiner, or a control freak. I see some leaders wear that "control freak" badge with honour. Tragically, it is a fear-based behaviour that only blocks you from interacting with trust, respect, love, and kindness.

I am not suggesting if you have experienced any form of abuse that you take responsibility for the abuse. You are not responsible for being on the receiving end. My invitation is for each of us to walk this journey to become more powerful with someone we trust like a therapist, your EAP (employee assistance program which is free if your organization has this program), a leadership coach, your pastor, or an outpatient or inpatient shelter. My philosophy is that you deserve to work with people who are specialized and have years of experience under their belts to guide and support you.

Until the abuse has stopped or been worked through you will find yourself in a raw place and may feel like you are spinning your wheels in the mud. Make yourself a priority and seek help. I can't tell you the number of leaders I have worked with who say, "That was in the past, Cate. I'm over it." Or "I had a fabulous childhood. No issues." However, past. The wreckage of their past oozes into their everyday life. If they felt invisible in their childhood home, they often made their feelings disappear too, bottling them up until one day the top blows off, leaving them no choice but to deal with it.

It is human nature to wait until you hit a crisis to actually deal with the past, however so much damage control could be avoided, and resolve could occur if you faced it head on before the eruption. I'm not saying look under every rock and psychoanalyze every part of your childhood. I am suggesting you create space in your life and schedule to focus on the patterns of power loss and power control behaviours. The truth of who you are and how you operate will surface. Be loving and kind with yourself as you complete this discovery work. Create a power team of supporters around you who are willing to tell you the truth about your part in a situation, lean on each other, do reality checks, and remind you of the power of who you truly are.

Taking full responsibility also applies to your staff, your adult children, your spouse, your siblings, a parent, and any adult relationship you are engaged in. You didn't become a leader once you graduated or received training. You likely were a leader in your family of origin as well. Helping others is likely a big part of who you are. It is one of your gifts or strengths. But like any strength that becomes amplified, it can turn into a shortcoming. Have you ever jumped in to support someone in your life when in actuality it was their responsibility? You may have listened to them vent again, helped them pay off debt again, supported them through another bad relationship again, or some other form of helping. Helping can be the sunny side of control.

Part of maintaining your optimum health and performance as a powerhouse leader is to ask yourself, "Who is responsible for this?" I like to use the image of a hula hoop. You are responsible for your thoughts, feelings, and actions within the hula hoop. Outside your hula hoop is beyond your control and not your responsibility. This approach allows you to focus your time, energy, and money on what you are responsible for. This act of detaching with love frees up all parties to live with the consequences of their actions and avoid repeating history.

When I found myself in this web of helping someone who either didn't ask for my help or clearly could figure out what to do next, I realized that I robbed them of taking full responsibility for their choices.

What Unique Qualities Do You Bring to Your Leadership?

In my experience a common cause of stress is forgetting to do things your way and forgetting to show up as you are meant to be.

It's easy to get so bogged down in following the flock or lost in the process that you lose sight of why they hired you in the first place. If you are feeling stressed out or overwhelmed likely your talents and gifts have been squandered. Creativity is one of my strengths. If I am mired down in a project and my energy is getting depleted, I quickly check in with how bringing more creativity to the project will help me perform at my peak. Exercise 2 will help you to step into or remember your purpose.

Exercise 2
STEPPING INTO YOUR PURPOSE

At the top of a blank page, make a list of five qualities (minimum) that you bring to the table as a leader. Ask trusted colleagues, friends, and family what qualities they admire in you. My clients report back how pleasantly surprised they were to hear the feedback. It warmed their hearts to know the people that mattered most to them saw them in this light. Be sure to have quality traits that do not end in "ing." I will explain later. For example, organized, integrity, good communicator, empathic, authentic, good listener, compassionate or intelligent.

Circle the top three qualities that you think best describe you based on your findings from others and yourself.

Now write each of these qualities on another blank piece of paper on the left side of your page, leaving lots of space between them. Then add three action words (ending in "ing") that describe how you demonstrate that quality. Make sure you have nine different action words in the end. Keep it simple.

▶ *Example*

Good communicator – communicating, listening, responding
Integrity – respecting, hardworking, dedicating
Playful – playing, joking, story telling

Once completed, at the top of a blank piece of paper write, "My purpose as an effective and powerhouse leader is to be (fill in your three circled qualities and then include your nine action words).

▶ *Example*

My purpose as an effective and powerhouse leader is to be a good communicator, playful and use my integrity through communicating, listening, responding, respecting, working hard, dedicating, playing, joking, and telling stories.

Now read your purpose statement out loud. This is your true north compass.

If you were hired for your playfulness or your creativity in your leadership role, your spirit will struggle with energy, clarity, and peace of mind when you are not using your gifts or talents. When you are not in alignment with your purpose you can feel more like a human doer versus a human being.

With this purpose or vision statement your Four-Room house is solid and secure. This becomes the filter that brings clarity on what to say yes to and what to say no to. It allows you to be in alignment with your purpose of why you are here. We have all had those times when we said yes to something and later regretted that decision. Inside you knew that it was not the best use of your time. The clearer you become about your purpose and using this true north compass, the easier it will be to pause and assess whether this commitment, event, or person brings you closer or further away from your goals or dreams. "Does the thought of this commitment or person inspire me or expire me?"

This may sound a little morbid but think about laying on your death bed. You don't want to have regrets. Will you be saying, "I'm so glad I spent all that time on that committee because of all the good we did for that community." Or will you be saying, "I wish I'd spent more time with my family because they needed me." For me, prior to drifting off to sleep and exiting this world, I will be reminiscing about how grateful I am for living my purpose of reminding people who they truly are and to be that powerhouse they are meant to be coupled with being present for my family.

Think about your end result and work backwards.

Think about your end result and work backwards. What do you want to be remembered for as a leader? Then act accordingly now, not when a tragedy occurs. It is easy to get caught up in the day-to-day operations. Keeping your purpose statement close by will guide you. You may put it on a cue card and take a photo of it or have it on all your technology. You would be surprised at how many powerhouse leaders use this purpose statement, or something similar, to skyrocket their results.

When you are connected to your purpose and why you are here, everyone around you feels the difference. They see the shift in how you show up for them. There is a heart and head connection, you are more present and more pleasant to be around rather than having fear as your driver to get things done.

How You Start Your Day, Shapes Your Day

A great way to maintain this much needed self-awareness of how you respond, along with centering or grounding yourself before you jump into your busy day, is to have a daily routine.

How you start your day, shapes your day. I recommend a Power of Four Practice (See Figure 1 and Exercise 3).

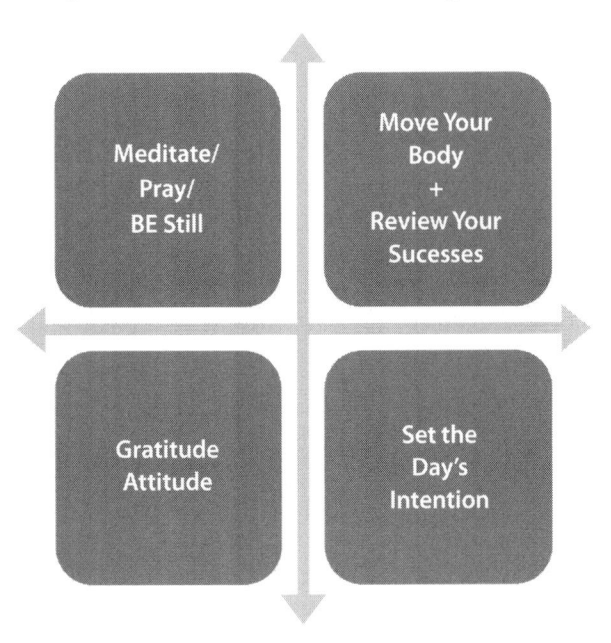

Figure 1: **The Power of Four Morning Practice**

Meditate/ Pray/ BE Still	Move Your Body + Review Your Sucesses
Gratitude Attitude	Set the Day's Intention

Schedule time in your morning, before your coffee and opening your laptop, to do the following.

1. **Meditate or Pray or Be Still**

   Find a chair, preferably in your bedroom, and spend anywhere from 5 to 30 minutes meditating. Many successful leaders, including Arianna Huffington from Huffington Post, meditate for 30 minutes before starting their day.

2. **Move Your Body and Review Your Successes**

   Fifteen to thirty minutes of Yoga, Pilates, brisk walking or going to your gym will release any tension and wake up the endorphins in your body. Kickstarting your fitness regime with morning workouts will help you build muscle faster especially on an empty stomach. And it's all thanks to your hormones. In the early hours of the day, levels of vital hormones that build muscle mass, like testosterone, are higher. By exercising in the morning, you can take advantage of this. I like to combine reviewing my successes or wins in the previous 24 hours to remind myself of the powerhouse I am. You are building your body's muscles and your confidence muscles at the same time.

3. **Gratitude Attitude**

    Journal or reflect on what specifically you are grateful for and how you can act and share this gratitude. With gratitude in your heart and thoughts, there is no room for fear and apprehension. Remember what the English poet, artist, and mystic, William Blake, said, "Gratitude is heaven itself."

4. **Set the Day's Intention**

    How do you want to show up? You may have an important meeting, a courageous conversation, or a decision you need to make. Being the best version of yourself is important. Perhaps you want to be fully present, confident, be clear and concise, or you may need to set a boundary. When you get your head in the game beforehand, your body will follow. Your brain is like a computer, when you input the decision to show up and come from confidence, love, or a desire to serve, your words, your actions, and especially your body language will follow. Starting your day with this powerful routine will set the tone for your day.

Exercise 3
POWER OF FOUR MORNING ROUTINE

Commit to doing the Power of Four Morning Practice for 21 days (see Figure 1).
 Observe or write about your new-found peace, confidence, focus, and calmness to start your day.

Navigating so many decisions, crises, different personalities, and needs throughout your day will conjure up many different thoughts and responses and checking into your Mentally Fit Room daily will help.

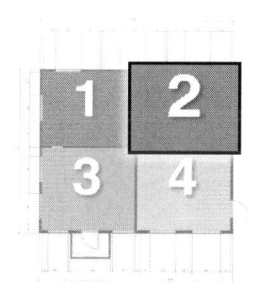

Room Two

YOUR EMOTIONALLY FIT ROOM

The second of the Four Rooms is your Emotionally Fit Room. It follows your Mentally Fit Room, because your thoughts and your emotions have a complex relationship and are very connected.

Your emotions often take cues from your thoughts. Think about a time when you felt overwhelmed and stressed and your thoughts kept repeating, "I am never going to get all of this done. I am so stressed." Did you feel energized and hopeful? Or exhausted and discouraged?

You can see the connection between your Mentally Fit Room and this Room. When your heart is right, your world is right.

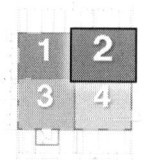

Chapter 5

Feel Your Feelings – Feelings Are Not Facts

Feelings are simply information – not good nor bad. Your feelings matter. When you acknowledge your feelings, accept them, and then let them go, freedom follows.

Admit Your Feelings

Your feelings are a part of you and need to be expressed. When they come knocking at your door of awareness its important you let them in. They say pain is inevitable, but suffering is optional. Learning how to pay attention to your feelings without being tormented by them will serve you well in your leadership role. When you neglect to feel your feelings, it sets you up for a fall.

Treat yourself with the same care and respect you would a friend, colleague, employee, or someone you serve.

For me, to say that my Emotionally Fit Room was out of shape was an understatement. I was drowning in all my unrealistic expectations of myself to fully show up for everyone in my life. It was in this emotional breaking point that I needed to let Super Woman leave the building (or in today's world, Wonder Woman). It was only when I gave myself permission

---

Tap into the great wisdom within you. For more powerful exercises and solutions for your Emotionally Fit Room, visit my website: https://powerfuljourney.com/emotionallyfitroom

to feel powerless at that very vulnerable time in my life that I was able to take my power back.

My stress leave was not very popular with my boss, nor my doctor, but my warrior within made it a non-negotiable. During that time of healing and therapy, I was able to step off the stress treadmill and uncover how I felt. Perhaps you know and connect with your feelings regularly. At that time, I did not.

Thanks to a patient and loving therapist I was able to observe the patterns in my life. Rather than feel what I deserved to feel, I unconsciously jumped into "fix others" mode.

I would easily feel outrage, hurt, sadness, or rejection for someone else's circumstance, only to discover in therapy that I was often projecting how I felt. The little Cate within me felt invisible. She felt discounted. She felt unimportant. She felt sad and alone. She also felt angry that I would spend so much time trying to be a warrior for other people when there was an inner war going on within me.

Can you relate? Do you have a tendency to make the feelings of your clients or patients or teams more important than your feelings? I have heard clients say, "I know, but my hurt is nothing compared to what _____ has experienced." Or "I know that we all have had difficult times in our lives," effectively dismissing their feelings. Or "I don't have time right now?"

Imagine for a moment that you put an uncovered bowl of applesauce in your fridge. You have every intention of removing it, but life is busy. You move that uncovered applesauce around and finally to the back of your fridge, so you don't have to see it. Weeks pass by or, depending on how busy you are, months. When you decide to take the bowl of uncovered applesauce out of the fridge, it is still there. It hasn't gone anywhere. It is buried under the furry, smelly stuff, but it is still there.

Your feelings are much like that. Pretending they aren't there won't make them go away. If you are like me and you wait until numbness and despair kick in, it will take more time to dig down to locate the applesauce.

Keep in mind that regardless of where you are in your leadership journey in relation to your Emotionally Fit Room, this is a Room that requires your attention. At the core of every human being we need to feel safe. If you choose to neglect this part of yourself, it will manifest in other ways. What you don't talk about and feel will show up in your body through aches and pains, cancer, and other illnesses (see Your Physically Fit Room).

Many of the female leaders I work with share how they have followed the example set by their female role models – putting other people's needs and feelings above their own.

Please learn from my burn out experience and choose another path. Put yourself on the top of your list. The flight attendant informs you to put your mask on first and then put the mask on the loved one beside you. You can't be of any use to them if you are dead.

Feel Your Feelings

Now that we've let our feelings in, we need to delve a little deeper and learn to let them go. If feelings are something you have little experience with or were not allowed to feel when you were a child, hang in there. Here are some tried and true methods for digging into those feelings and then letting them go.

Put Pen to Paper

I am a huge fan of journaling. Whether you do this daily or when certain feelings surface, I have found huge benefits both for my clients and myself.

It is a great way to pour out onto paper what you are feeling. Beneath the feeling of anger frequently lurks hurt, rejection, sadness, or frustration that someone is violating your boundaries. By writing it out, you will find any underlying emotions (see Exercise 4).

Exercise 4

SEND IT OFF IN A LETTER

Write a letter to the person or situation you are upset about, but don't send it to them. This allows you to hold nothing back and tell the full truth about how you feel.

If you prefer brief notes, keep a pad of paper close by to jot down bullet points of what you are feeling at that moment.

Scheduling in regular "me time" to check in with yourself will help connect you with how you feel and what and who will best support those feelings.

Make an Emotional Debrief Plan

What first comes to mind when you think of a debrief plan? Following a disaster or traumatic event, like a fire or a car accident, emergency first responders are debriefed to learn more from an event – what worked, what didn't, and how to learn and improve in the future.

In this case, I am referring to your emotional debrief plan following a major deadline, team or family crisis (death, major conflict, divorce, mental health issues, addiction), or any number of stressful situations you experience in your organization. Too often, the norm in organizations is "Next." You and your team have poured all your reserve energy into completing a project. Now, before you've had time to come up for air, you have to move on to the next deadline. Building in some reflection time is not seen as a priority by most organizations.

Creating a debrief plan is a healthy investment to maintain the powerhouse leader in you. The constant stress you experience as a leader compounds over time. This prevention strategy helps you avoid major meltdowns or emotional crises later. What you don't give yourself permission to feel – the unresolved emotions – manifests in your body.

> *What you don't give yourself permission to feel – the unresolved emotions – manifests in your body.*

What debrief plan do you practice following a crisis? Do you build in time to rest, connect with nature, engage in spiritual practices, share with a trusted friend or colleague, or book a soothing massage? What if you scheduled this during *and* after the completion of your deadline or project?

Discovering who you are includes asking yourself different questions. Are you highly sensitive? Do your feelings get hurt easily?

Here's another thought, what if your high sensitivity is a form of conceit – deep down you think you are the focus of other people's actions. Ouch, right? "You aren't that important, Cate," my mentor shared while helping me leave a volunteer role where I felt tremendous guilt. "Somehow, they managed before you came to the committee, and somehow they will manage without you." Reality check.

Where are you taking on unnecessary responsibility for others? Your clients or family or colleague or boss or spouse or child or friend? What is the emotional toll? Building in time to step away from your life or step away from your role will help you take that necessary pause so you can take better emotional care of yourself. Check in with yourself in Exercise 5.

Exercise 5

CHECKING IN

On a scale from one to ten, how would you rate yourself in regard to consistently checking in with yourself about how you feel and what you need?

1   2   3   4   5   6   7   8   9   10

What number would you like to be? Although ten may be the ideal, let's look at shifting you a few numbers over to keep it manageable.

What action steps will you take to shift that number higher?

_____

_____

_____

_____

For me, after I meditate, I try to check in with myself about how I am feeling. This gives me insight as to what I need that day. I may not be able to journal right then however I can commit to doing that later that day.

Feeling Safe – At Our Very Cores

As mentioned earlier, at the core of each one of us we need to know we are safe. Most of our fears and anxiety stem from this place of insecurity. If you are someone who received reassurance from your parents that no matter how horrible your life was going, you would eventually be not just okay, but you'd thrive, then you are one of the lucky ones. That sense of hope and faith was never instilled in many people, especially for people where abuse and addiction were a part of their family upbringing.

When it appears that one of your staff is overreacting to a situation, there is a high probability they have been triggered from their past. It's like having a house built with no solid foundation. Remember how the three little pigs built three houses of different materials. Then the big bad wolf blows down the first two pigs' houses made of straw and sticks, but is unable to destroy the third pig's house, which was made of bricks.

We want to focus on ensuring your leadership house is solid, able to weather any storm or big bad wolf. That big bad wolf can be fear of any number of things, including job loss, performance reviews, backstabbing and gossip, not being good enough, serious illness or death of a loved one, or the fear they will finally figure out you don't have any idea what you are doing. When you don't take the time to become aware of what your triggers are to feel safe, you leave yourself vulnerable.

Within you is a vulnerable or wounded child, a punitive parent, a rebellious teenager, and of course a loving woman or man. These parts of you have become fragmented and feel disconnected when you are feeling unsafe. The next time you feel off, anxious, or stressed, repeat this affirmation, "I am safe." You will be surprised by the calm and peace that washes over you. Inhaling "I am" and exhaling "safe" is also powerful. Another response is, "All is well. Everything serves. And for the highest good of all."

A friend shared with me an effective prompt – H.A.L.T.E. It stands for Hungry, Angry, Lonely, Tired, or haven't had Exercise (see Figure 2). When it occurs your emotions can go astray. If you are experiencing any one of these conditions, you must take care of them first in order to make a decision. Otherwise you can expect to overreact to something or someone and say or do the wrong thing, and then have to perform damage control later. Emotions destroy intelligence when we don't keep them in check.

Some of my clients come to me on autopilot. They had spent years denying anger, joy, or sadness for a variety of reasons. Some come from alcoholic, abusive, or undiagnosed mental illness in their homes and others come from homes where perfectionism was expected. Survival was the only thing on their minds. I remind them that they have feelings. At first it was uncomfortable for them because it was foreign. As long as you keep your feelings trapped inside, they will become poisonous secrets. You have heard the phrase, "Your secrets keep you sick." Once you understand what you are feeling, you are better equipped to deal with them.

As a leader in the human service field, you see all too often how post-traumatic stress, secondary trauma, and burn out are major hazards among your colleagues. Perhaps there are signs you recognize that indicate that committing to a self-care plan is vital for your emotional well-being. When the people around you are breathing too loudly this may be an indicator you need some self-care. You can only fake it until you make it for so long. Eventually it catches up to you.

Figure 2: **H.A.L.T.E.**

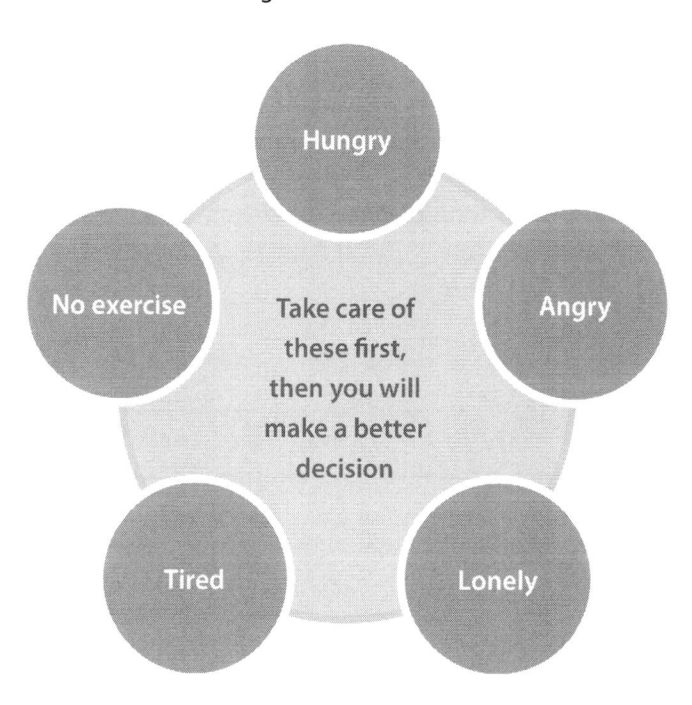

- Hungry
- Angry
- Lonely
- Tired
- No exercise

Take care of these first, then you will make a better decision

I have witnessed countless leaders neglect their Emotional Room because they think they don't have time to feel, or don't have time to focus on themselves when their clients or patients or staff are suffering. You are gifted at spotting the signs of burnout in your colleagues or your team – exhaustion, lack of focus, obsessing over things they can't control, withdrawing, not letting their needs be important, unrealistic expectations of themselves or others, angry outbursts, toxic interactions with others (like blaming, gossiping), problem focused in their conversations, crying outbursts, etc. – and yet it's hard to spot in yourself. By committing to checking into your Emotionally Fit Room regularly you will be more confident, more relaxed, experience greater peace of mind, and be a more authentic leader. We really do teach what we need to know the most.

Figure 3 provides a feelings chart that will help guide you with what you are feeling. You don't know what you don't know. This will help you be able to name what you are feeling.

Figure 3: **Feelings Chart**

| Happy | Joyful | Content | Silly | Sad | Angry |
| Scared | Worried | Confused | Surprised | Hurt | Embarrassed |

With this awareness you can figure out your next right step. Next let's explore the emotion that causes us the most difficulty, can be quite complex, and spreads into other emotions and reactions – yep, it's guilt.

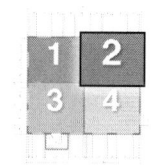

Chapter 6

Freedom from Guilt

Let's differentiate between shame and guilt. Shame says, "I am bad." Guilt says, "I did something bad."

When you have feelings of guilt, notice where it shows up in your body?

For me it's around my heart. It's as if someone is pressing on my heart. I know that if I gossip or judge another, guilt shows up there. I am reminded that I am not coming from love and that I need to course correct. I may need to apologize to someone for something I said/didn't say, or it may be changing my behaviour in the future. If I promise myself that I will take a much-needed walk on my lunch break and I renege on myself, guilt shows up. I feel guilty for not following through on what I said I would do to practice self-care.

Tripping on Guilt

Stop guilt tripping yourself. Stop blaming yourself for not knowing what you didn't know. Stop feeling guilty for not getting it all done. Stop revisiting the laundry list of people and things you still haven't taken care of. Stop hanging yourself out to dry.

Frequently the things you feel guilty about are not even your issues. They may stem from an overtaxed organization, unrealistic views of how working mothers should show up for their families, and misconceptions about how women should "suck up" all the different roles they are

---

Tap into the great wisdom within you. For more powerful exercises and solutions for your Emotionally Fit Room, visit my website: https://powerfuljourney.com/emotionallyfitroom

responsible for. And for the men, your pressure may include being a good provider for your family, being a rock, and "sucking up" any emotions that don't include anger.

Guilt robs you of your joy. It robs you of living fully in the precious present. Guilt prevents you from setting healthy boundaries. Let's scrutinize a typical example. Your job description gets stretched beyond recognition when your organization is financially stretched and you, along with your team, are expected to do more with less. The massive list of things to do are unrealistic for you to complete in one day, two days, or even a week with all the distractions, crises, and events happening at work. At some point it is vital to get back to the basics of your primary role as a leader as opposed to the unrealistic expectations you keep piling on yourself.

> *Guilt robs you of your joy. It robs you of living fully in the precious present.*

Setting Boundaries

Jan hired me to facilitate a team retreat for her organization. She later hired me for leadership coaching for herself.

She was a very seasoned competent manager who loved what she did. She believed in the core values of her organization and the tremendous impact her staff were making on their communities. Lately though, she felt guilty and incompetent most of the time because her leadership role kept getting tested by yet another committee, another proposal, another meeting, another policy that she was being asked to tackle by her CEO. When I was able to hold up a mirror for her with all the unrealistic expectations she was heaping on herself, she was able to come up for air and realize that her superior was treating her the way she treated herself. She could see that this vicious guilt cycle was turning into a shame cycle. The more she became unavailable to her staff, the more guilt she felt – and the dance continued.

It was clear that she needed to set a boundary with her boss. To Jan's surprise, her boss received this conversation very well and had been feeling similarly. They scheduled a meeting where they would redefine her role. Through a process of elimination, they reduced her to-do list so Jan could focus on her top priorities rather than feeling scattered and incompetent. This healthy boundary saved her a ton of guilt and future grief.

This is a great example of how coaching or sharing with someone you trust can breathe a new perspective on a challenge you may be having. Try Exercise 6 if you feel you need to set a boundary. Often, we can't see the forest for the trees.

Exercise 6
SETTING A BOUNDARY

Write down who or what you need to let go of.

_____

Considering this person/situation, write out how you plan to let go. Be specific.

"I am letting go of feeling responsible for _____ 's health and well-being. I set them free."

My action step is _____ by

_____

_____

_____

Ask someone you trust to hold you accountable for taking this action of setting your boundary. When guilt pops its head in, ask yourself, "Who is responsible for this?

Sharing your responses with a trusted mentor helps.

Guilt Is a Thing of the Past

Guilt also prevents you from practicing self-care. Guilt is a burden that keeps you from giving yourself fully and freely to the present. You can begin to rid your mind of guilt by admitting where and when you truly have done something wrong to people in your life or yourself.

"Sorry I forgot your birthday." "Sorry I missed our appointment." Then move on. Choose acceptance and peace. Avoid chaining yourself to the past of self-defeating guilt or by exaggerating the importance of your mistakes. Instead face your past head on, heal your wounds, and move forward into a carefree and happier life today.

Ask yourself, "What would I be thinking instead if I chose acceptance and peace?" You are imperfect. So am I. It is when you truly accept that about yourself that you feel freedom. Embrace your humanness. Own your humanness. Accept your humanness with all its imperfections. It all starts with a choice. Choose wisely. When you treat yourself with kindness versus guilt tripping yourself, others will follow suit. How you choose to treat yourself shows up in all your relationships.

Taking a walk in nature helps remove me from the situation and get a better detached view of the situation. I return to the situation with a new and refreshed perspective.

In Don Miguel Ruiz's book, *The Four Agreements,* agreement #2 states, "Don't take anything personal."[13] What people say and do to you is a reflection on them, not you. Know who you are, and you won't take things personally.

What about how others try to guilt trip you? I bet you have stories where you felt hostage to people who manipulated, whined, coerced, persuaded, and who spent loads of time investing in your commitment to take care of them. These are people who don't love themselves. And they are also amazing teachers. These are people who come into your life to remind you that you are responsible for you and they are responsible for themselves.

Take a moment and look into the future. If you continue doing what you are doing for them (enabling), you will continue getting what you are getting. Why would they need to change if you keep showing up and taking care of things for them? Makes you ask, "How is this serving me?" which leads us deeper into our Emotionally Fit Room.

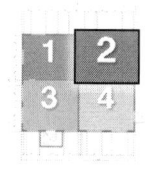

Chapter 7

Let Go of What Isn't Serving You and Forgive

How many times have you experienced illness or the death of a loved one, or a mental health issue with a family member, friend, or yourself, and still expected yourself to pull up your bootstraps and carry on at work as if nothing had happened? We wouldn't expect it from a team member or someone else, and yet we expect it from ourselves. What's up with that?

I question whether our society has mistaken strong leadership with wearing a suit of armour that prevents you from feeling and being a human. When a crisis occurs, letting go of some of your responsibilities is healthy.

A friend and colleague, Lila Larson,[14] always says, "Up Until Now!" Thinking like "I am a control freak," "I am hypersensitive," "I always put others' needs ahead of my own," or "I have always done it this way" gets interrupted when you use the phrase, "up until now." You shift your language and mindset to focus more on the solution instead of the problem. I have used this phrase for many years now. The power of these three words interrupts that old way of thinking and allows me to step into the power of who I am and who I am meant to be.

Tap into the great wisdom within you. For more powerful exercises and solutions for your Emotionally Fit Room, visit my website: https://powerfuljourney.com/emotionallyfitroom

What Letting Go Looks Like

Letting go may include looking at situations where you take on responsibility for other people's choices. For me it was a process. I have learned that I need to give others the dignity to make their own choices without my permission. I had no idea when I was busy in their business that I was stunting their growth. Ironic, right? The very help I was giving was, in fact, hurting them not helping them.

Naturally there are times when you need to step up to the plate and support the people who matter most in your life. The key is asking yourself, "What is *my motive* here? What is *my intention*? If it is to change them, if it is to take over, then you are robbing them of taking ownership for their choices and their life and ultimately robbing them of their power.

Self-examination for what you need to let go of on a weekly basis will be important for you more than ever with the current mental health crisis. Being a good mentor and coach for your team is top of mind these days and unheard of ten years ago.

Part of this letting go involves knowing who you are and what your strengths and shortcomings are. At the heart of being a powerhouse leader is to know your own limits. Even with my extensive counselling background, I knew that when I was working with a client who was suicidal, I needed to refer them to the hospital immediately. If I was working with a client who shared they were being abused by their partner, I referred them to a shelter. I couldn't be all the things my clients needed because it was not my area of expertise or within my mandate.

There was a time when employees knew to check their personal lives at home. Now, they're encouraged to bring their integrated self to work. As a leader, you juggle so many responsibilities, and now you can add employee mental health issues, which are on the rise. Being clear about what is within your wheelhouse and your job description is critical. Otherwise, you will take home all the problems, challenges, and crises of your staff. Of course, supporting your team perform at their best includes being that beacon of hope by listening and being patient and kind, however letting them take full responsibility for their life and their choices is key. Your human resource professional will be equipped to make appropriate referrals for your employee.

Letting go can be difficult if being in control is a priority (see Exercise 7). Being willing to try to let go is a start. I am one of those people who likes to be in control. Have you experienced situations where you felt out of control?

Brené Brown says, "We don't talk about the hustle for worthiness that's become such a part of our lives that we don't even realize that we're dancing."[15]

Exercise 7
BREATHE IT OUT

Where are you currently heaping expectations on yourself that are unrealistic?
Let go. Let's do this together. In this moment, right now, let go.
Take in a deep inhale and say, "I *am*" and then exhale *"worthy."*
Do this exercise until at your core you believe it.
Anxiety, fear, and worry only compound, like the interest on your credit card bill, when you don't take that moment to face it head on.

Many of my clients come to me filled with fear that if they truly let go, humpty dumpty will not be put back together again. He will, I promise. You have been here before. Maybe in a milder way, or maybe worse, however you did get through it. The only way through it, is by going through it. Let your walls come down and stop trying to be perfect all the time. Let go of needing to control every area of your life, let go of trying to be everything for everyone else, let go of holding yourself responsible for what others do or don't do, let go of trying to be the peacekeeper, let go of being the leader in every area of your life and especially let go of being so hard on yourself. When you make the decision to let go, you breathe peace into your spirit.

Letting go means staying in the present moment, which is all you have. Letting go means trusting that everything – absolutely everything – is happening exactly as it is supposed to. What letting go means is getting out of your head and getting into your heart. Let super woman or wonder woman or superman leave the building.

Life is about ebbs and flows. Letting go means stepping away from the debating society in your head. Letting go means giving up control. Letting go means deep down you know – even if it's only a small glimmer of belief – that you are worthy enough. Letting go means attending to your mental, emotional, physical, and spiritual needs like you would a small child. Letting go means being vulnerable to the truth that you are supported, loved, and cared for by your Higher Power. Letting go means drinking in the truth that you are totally enough right now without exceptions.

Permitting Yourself to Let Go

What methods do you use to give yourself permission to let go?

For some it's writing in a journal, getting a massage, yoga or Pilates, doing breath work, sitting by water, meditating, having a hot soak or shower, church, playing like a child, belly laughing, sex, crying, hugging, sharing with someone close, watching your favourite TV program, connecting with Mother Nature. The variety is as diverse as we are.

As your shoulders relax, your breath becomes deeper, and you are fully in the present.

That employee who has not been delivering quality services even with support and accommodations, who is a constant disruptor and creates unnecessary conflict or drama for your team needs to be written up. Being compassionate and empathetic to others is a genuine strength as a leader, but if you lose sight of who owns the problem you may be working much harder than they are at trying to course correct. If they are not willing to put skin in the game to change things, then you have now taken ownership of their problem versus them. You do them a great disservice.

If they need to sit in their problem longer and reap what they sow, this is all part of their journey. Not everyone is ready to make necessary changes. Your role as a leader is to provide a safe environment for them by giving them the tools to perform their duties, consistent clear communication to connect them to your organization's core values, accountability, opportunities to collaborate with their peers, and inspiring messages to support and motivate them. You can bring the horse to the water but you can't make it drink. Someone's resistance to change may cost them a relationship, their health, their self-esteem, or their work performance (even their job), however, in the end, ultimately the responsibility lies with them. Let go of the outcome and focus on your part and your responsibility. It is enough. You are enough.

Holding yourself and others accountable is part of your leadership role.

Holding yourself and others accountable is part of your leadership role. It may be hard, nevertheless it is necessary.

Forgiveness Begins with a Decision

As we know, forgiveness is a huge area that deserves much more time than what I am able to devote to it in this book. I encourage you to seek out resources to support you. When you think of all the hours, months, and possibly years you wasted feeding that hurt or resentment only to have it harm you the most. In Chapter 1, we explored the question "Have You Given Your Power Away?" Forgiveness requires time and energy. I highly recommend working with a therapist if you are ready to begin your forgiveness journey.

Depending on the depth of the forgiveness, you deserve to pace yourself. Sometimes, one hurt or resentment may trigger other resentments and your response may be huge. Pay attention to that and proceed with care. This healing takes time, but remember that your reward is you get your power back.

It all starts with a decision. Once you make the decision to forgive and put your past in the past, you will be surprised by what shifts in you. Staying willing to figure this out is key. There will be times when you don't have a clue what to do. That is normal. Stay the course. Often buried resentment can explode at the oddest times. Typically, when any of us are in an unsettled state or in conflict with someone, we tend to be defensive, fearful, and angry.

People you love have made mistakes. You have likely wrestled with forgiveness at some point in your life – either being forgiven or forgiving someone else. As an article from Neurocore Brain Performance Centers indicates, forgiveness can be good for your health.[16]

> A study from Emory University found that bitter people had higher blood pressure and were more likely to die from heart disease than more forgiving people.
>
> This could be due to something called a C-reactive protein, which has been linked to heart disease and stroke. When we experience negative feelings (which can be brought on by conflict), our bodies get ready to fight. Staying in that "fight" state for an extended period of time can increase the amount of C-reactive protein in our bloodstreams, potentially increasing the likelihood of heart disease.
>
> On top of that, prolonged feelings of resentment can also negatively impact metabolism, immune response, and organ function. Those feelings also put you at a higher risk of developing depression and anxiety.

Additionally, Louise Hay shares that, "Cancer is a deep hurt. Long-standing resentment. Deep secret or grief eating away at the self. Carrying hatreds."[17]

There are some misconceptions about forgiveness. Let's explore what forgiveness isn't. Forgiveness doesn't mean the action or behaviour is forgotten. Forgiveness isn't about making what you did to me acceptable. Nor does it mean you are inviting them to do it again.

Forgiveness means that you are no longer willing to carry around those boulders of pain in response to their actions. As long as you hold unforgiveness in your heart, the more you punish yourself. As long-time radio host, Bernard Meltzer once said, "When you forgive, you in no way change the past, but you sure do change the future."

As you have discovered, I am a huge fan of rating scales. So, on a scale of 1 to 10, what number would you rate yourself for being willing to consider forgiveness of someone? If you are at two, what would it take to shift two numbers up that scale? What would need to happen for you to be willing to set yourself free? Keep in mind that forgiveness does not mean the other person takes responsibility nor apologizes for their actions. This exercise is to set you free.

You have been drinking the poison all this time and expecting the other person to die. The longer you keep drinking it, the sicker you will become. When you have deep-rooted hurt, rejection, anger, and resentment it creates a domino effect through all your relationships.

If trust was broken, you will struggle with trusting others or yourself. If it was betrayal, then trust is part of that too. You may unconsciously create a similar situation that brings you feelings of mistrust.

Remember Exercise 1 (in Chapter 1), where I asked you to write a list of all the people and behaviours you've given your power away to. Let's take a deeper look at how you have harmed yourself and forgive yourself (see Exercise 8).

Exercise 8

FORGIVING YOURSELF

Warning: *Just a friendly reminder that participating in these exercises may bring up buried feelings. I highly recommend working with a therapist, coach, or trusted mentor. If you are feeling fragile at this time feel free to skip this exercise. This will be an act of self-love, not skipping out on an exercise. You know best.*

Write a letter (preferably with pad and pen) to your younger self. Begin with you as a small child and progress right up until who you are today. Let yourself get lost in this exercise. Start with a small forgiveness and let the hurt peel away like an onion.

Let me show you what I mean.

▶ *Example*

Dear Self,

I am sorry for all the times when I let you down. When I accepted unacceptable behaviour from _____.

I am sorry for abandoning you all those times I made _____'s problems and life more important than mine.

I am deeply sorry for obsessing over people, places, and things that I had no control over instead of making you a priority.

I am deeply sorry for giving away my power to _____ by retraumatizing myself, by retelling my story over and over again about how I was a victim instead of putting my focus on healing.

I am deeply sorry for squashing your dreams of _____ and desires for _____ when I listened to my inner critic instead of believing in what I know to be true – that I am capable, I am worthy, and I am enough.

I am deeply sorry for pretending that my feelings of anger, sadness, worry, my pain, my experiences don't matter. They do matter. I matter.

My commitment moving forward is to make you a priority by checking in daily on how you feel, becoming more aware of what you need from me or others, by fully accepting and loving you now, not when something is achieved, but now. I am your greatest fan and plan to prove it to you every day.

All my love,

Me xo

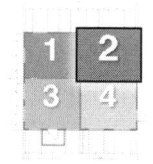

Chapter 8

Setting Healthy Boundaries

As women, we are conditioned to nurture others, but that very strength often turns against you when it comes to nurturing yourself. Having clear boundaries will give you the energy and confidence to explore more of who you are and what opportunities you would like to engage in.

Think of a time when you already felt swallowed up by all your commitments and ended up volunteering for yet another responsibility or obligation. Did you think to yourself, "What was I thinking? I'm already drowning in all that I have to do."

Get Honest About Priorities

Owning your power as that powerhouse leader starts with getting honest about what your priorities are on that day, for that quarter, or that week in your life. Life as we know it is changing at astronomical speeds and in order to interrupt your old, unhealthy behaviours it will be important to pause. Sanity is within the pause. Knowing where you begin and where you end is important.

Knowing where you begin and where you end is important.

Having healthy boundaries will be easier once you are clear about your "why?" Why is it important this month that you spend time with

---

Tap into the great wisdom within you. For more powerful exercises and solutions for your Emotionally Fit Room, visit my website: https://powerfuljourney.com/emotionallyfitroom

your ill mother, your troubled child, your grieving heart, or any number of situations. Once you take that pause, clarity will follow.

Many of my clients have found that when they are on vacation, or they have vacated their life if only for an hour, a day, or a week, they are able to get clear about where they want to spend their time. If you are involved in a commitment that is sucking the life out of you, pay attention. Here are some questions that may help.

- Is it time to review how best you can serve?
- How is this commitment serving you best?
- What does your heart say?
- If you could change one thing about this commitment, what would it be?
- Who can help you with that?
- What do you need to be thinking, doing, and saying differently to get the result you want?

As managers and leaders, you are expected to be that powerful example for your team and your organization as a whole. Matching your talents and your strengths with the commitments is helpful. I realize you don't always get to choose. However, there may be a compromise within your thinking or the situation. Minimally, you get to choose the reframe.

Let's work through an example. You may be thinking, "I really don't like one of the people I am sitting on this committee with, however my boss has asked me to sit on the committee." Try these questions as a means to get clearer.

- What is your primary objective for being there? Get clear with your boss on this point.
- What specific expectations does he or she have for you sitting on the committee?
- Are you expected to attend every meeting?
- How important is this role in relation to your responsibilities within the organization?
- Is there movement to play at 70% versus 100% investment, given the current deadlines you and your organization are facing?

When you get busy it's easy to forget things are not black and white. Pausing and reflecting allows you to reassess whether this commitment is important under the current circumstances. While under constant stress, forgetting that you have a choice is common.

Talk to a breast cancer survivor or someone who has faced death or serious illness and they will say they shifted their priorities to make sure their health was at the top of their to-do list. Defining your identity and value by your position is a mistake. Keep in mind there is much more to you than that. Part of owning your power is to recognize that you have many talents, desires, dreams, interests, and relationships outside your work. Creating a healthy balance between your role and other areas in your life is key.

This leads me to my next point. If you are last on your list most days, this is a red flag. The only one who can change this is you. Even if you have to nudge yourself to take that walk, take a yoga class, honour your appointment with your weight trainer, go biking, or whatever activity you enjoy, follow through. Each time you do follow through expect to feel a rumbling of joy and happiness for making yourself a priority. There will be times you are dragging your heels because you would rather sit in front of the TV and veg out, but if you fast forward in your mind's eye you'll see how energized, how relaxed, how confident you feel following moving your body. Not exercising is a habit and it's a habit to exercise. The results however are very different.

To support you with your time management, Exercise 9 that will help you prioritize, delegate, and get clear about what needs to be eliminated. It is a mind map that I write every Monday morning to capture all my goals and responsibilities for the week on one page. It gives me a snapshot of what my priorities need to be, and it fast-tracks what I need to eliminate for that week or a particular day in order for me to achieve my goals.

Exercise 9
MONDAY MORNING MIND MAP

1. Take out a blank piece of paper and put a circle in the middle of the page about 2 inches in diameter.
2. Inside that circle write the date. I like to add how I want to show up around the circle.
3. Draw straight lines coming out from it (much like spokes attached to the wheel of a car).
4. Write all your commitments along each spoke.

▶ *Example*

I like to put things into categories with headings. For example, I usually have these categories listed separately: work, special project(s), family commitments, personal health and well-being commitments, service work (church, volunteering, mentoring), and general for things I'm not sure where they fit in the other spokes.

BUSINESS
- Contact _____ (past clients)
- Contact _____ (prospects)
- Prepare for a Leadership presentation
- Social media – 4 times/week
- Create a vlog (video blog)
- Prepare for coaching clients

BOOK (SPECIAL PROJECT)
- Email formatter
- Interview 2 book coaches
- Send title to designer

Clear, Concise, Playful, Abundant, Self-care, Aligned, Confident

AUGUST 10–16, 2020

PERSONAL
- Meditate daily (5–20 minutes)
- Drink 8 glasses of water
- Monday–Friday sugar free (processed)
- Eat vegetarian Monday–Friday
- Exercise (4 times/week):
  – walk & pilates
  – bike
  – gym
- Connect with Mother Nature 5–10 minutes daily
- Connect with my mentor
- Quality time with myself on Fridays
- Quality time with my husband on Thursdays
- Book a FaceTime call with grandkids

ASSISTANT
- Delegation list
- Social media updates
- Send out invoices
- Set up client calls
- Quickbooks entries

VOLUNTEER/SERVICE
- Mentor 2 female leaders (weekly)
- Read at church (2 times/week)
- Be present for whoever I connect with

5. Then walk away from this document. Go for a walk and connect with Mother Nature. Upon your return with fresh eyes, highlight or underline which areas you can delegate or write the letter D beside it.

When setting boundaries, you may find this list helpful to guide you.

1. What is my #1 priority in this moment, next week, or month?
2. As a filter, ask yourself, "How important is this task or responsibility right now in light of what is happening?"

3. What can I delegate? Who can support me here?
4. What can I decline or say I am not available for?
5. What would I choose, if I loved myself?
6. What no longer serves me or my team or organization?
7. Starting with the end result in mind, what will best support me to get there? For example, letting go of attending a certain meeting, delegating chores, meals, carpool, declining from hosting that dinner party and going out to eat instead, walking, or working out each morning to set the tone for my day.
8. *Add your own parameters.*

Let's say you have some serious deadlines you need to complete. Burning the candle at both ends may be what's needed for that short period of time.

The Flaw of Perfection

Remember a time when a loved one was sick, or a situation came up where you had to drop everything and go. Somehow your organization managed without you. Too often we guilt ourselves as leaders with needing to "do it all" that our thinking sets us up for exhaustion, resentment, disappointment, and discouragement. Delegating to staff or family means letting go of perfection. Your goal is to share the responsibilities, so everyone feels a part. Listen to their resistance and then set if free.

> *The key is treating yourself like you would a close friend.*

Combine activities. Call your mom when you take that much needed walk. Hire a house cleaner (could be your friend's teenager because it doesn't have to be perfect) during the high intensity tight deadlines. The key is treating yourself like you would a close friend. Expect less from yourself in other areas of your life so you can meet your deadline. Do you want to be completely used up at the end of your deadline or do you want to have some energy to spare for yourself to do the relaxing things that bring you joy? Being open and willing to try something different will open the door of possibilities. Sadly, when you don't take the time to plan ahead, once the project or deadline is completed, you find yourself home nursing a cold or flu because you spread yourself too thin and neglected to prioritize your time and commitments.

What blocks many leaders from setting healthy boundaries is their desire for control. I hear so many leaders say, "but I'm a control freak" or "I like to be in control." They wear it as a medal of distinction. There is a high price to pay when you maintain this distorted view of yourself. Being in control and using that control in ways that support you and those around you needs to focus on the common welfare of all involved. At the core of control is fear. When you don't discover what the fear is, control can wreak havoc on your relationships.

Being a powerhouse leader requires you to be in charge, however when you cross the line and become a nag or micro-manage, you defeat the purpose of your team working collaboratively. It starts at the top. When I was an executive director, I found being in control was a dance and I had to learn when to let go and when to take charge. When I lived my values, when I stayed true to my vision, and the vision of the organization, I focused my attention on the principles of why we were there instead of the personalities.

If in the past you had your power robbed from you this may have heightened your need for control. Ironically, you are striving for emotional safety and having rules to follow gives you the impression you will be safe, but the people around you feel the opposite. If you have ever been around someone who "does things this way" and has a lot of rules, it can be stifling. I know I make more mistakes around them because deep down I fear making a mistake or not doing the task to their high standards. When you lack flexibility and compassion for yourself as a leader, your team is left feeling insecure around you.

Being aware of this need for control is a great beginning; accepting that this was a survival tool from your past that may need adjusting takes time. (See Exercise 10 for help with delegating.) Focusing on what changes you want to make is important. Think about a time when you convinced yourself that someone was not playing by your rules only to find out there was a miscommunication. Is some of the feedback in your life that you have more rules than a sergeant in the army? Perhaps, the reason you crave control is you experienced a lack of control in a previous experience.

Sometimes a situation or person may trigger a previous time when you felt unsafe. Staying in the present and connected with how you feel will support you in making better decisions. Recognize how this need for control has tripped you up and caused you undue stress. Allow this to guide you in how you choose to act differently the next time. If you are always in control of everything, how does this impact other's growth? Does your need for control snuff out their learning? Making mistakes and not doing things your way will arise, however finding their own way to build their confidence is essential for healthy relationships.

Exercise 10
DELEGATION TO YOUR RESCUE

Where in your list of responsibilities can you let go and delegate to a team member or a family member to try their hand at it? It all starts with a decision.

Once you share with them your thoughts, spend time listening to what ideas they have and what they would like to implement, while keeping to the organization's or the family's vision.

▶ *Example*

Delegate the preparation of dinners to family members to free yourself up.
Delegate attending a particular meeting to a colleague or staff member who can share their notes with you later.

When you set healthier boundaries and have regular space in your calendar for you, it frees you up to pay attention to how you treat yourself in your thoughts and actions. Often when you are overwhelmed or are feeling emotionally depleted, it blocks you from connecting with limiting beliefs you have about yourself.

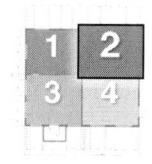

Chapter 9

Surround Yourself with Powerhouse People

Your Advisory Table

As a leader, in order to stay in your flow, stay in the high energy you need to perform well, stay in your wheelhouse of what you bring to the table and stay focused, it is important to do regular check-ins with yourself regarding who you allow at your table. Think of who is at the advisory table of a country's leaders. They have the brightest and best advisors at their table to inform, inspire, and tell them the truth of what is happening, so they make informed decisions.

Keep in mind each person plays a role. And no one person can provide you with everything you need. Each advisor comes with their own talents and strengths. I have a few close colleagues or mentors who I call on to tell me the truth of the situation. These advisors will help me find the eagle's eye view of the situation, especially when my emotions have run riot. I have a few close friends who I may see only once in a while, however we seem to pick up where we left off and have an open exchange.

What about you? Who is sitting at your advisor table? Do they inspire you or cause you to second guess yourself? Can you trust them? Who needs to stay and who needs to leave, if only for a while? I don't know about you, but I went through a period where I unconsciously projected

---

Tap into the great wisdom within you. For more powerful exercises and solutions for your Emotionally Fit Room, visit my website: https://powerfuljourney.com/emotionallyfitroom

onto people how they should show up for me. I mean it was obvious right? They should have got what I needed. Then I would need to take myself aside and remind myself that it is my responsibility to ask for what I needed. I am 100% responsible to speak my truth. I need to accept that the people at my advisor table may not be there forever. They may need to vacate their seat temporarily or permanently for different reasons. They may have gotten themselves into a negative place, felt exhausted and had nothing to give, or their purpose may have been support during a specific situation or event in my life.

I conduct an exercise (see Exercise 11) in my training and retreats that was inspired by a quote from Jim Rohn, American entrepreneur, author, and motivational speaker: "You are the average of the five people you spend the most time with."

Exercise 11
WHO DO YOU SPEND TIME WITH?

1. Write down the names of five people you spend the most time with, in a column with space between.
2. Put a check mark beside any of the people who may be critical of your dreams, mistakes, or who you are.
3. Circle the names who you can consistently count on to inspire you and remind you who you really are.
4. What are you pretending not to know with the person(s) who bring them down or critique what's wrong with them versus what is right?

   ▶ *Example*

   "I am pretending not to know that I deserve to be treated with respect and encouragement. I am pretending not to know that I matter. I am pretending not to know that my dreams, my challenges, or my life deserve to have an equal share. I am pretending not to know that I deserve to set a boundary. I am pretending not to know that this relationship no longer serves me. I am pretending not to know that this person is a psychic vampire. I am pretending not to know that I am not responsible for their life, they are. I am firing myself right now."

Conduct a Relationship Inventory

It's easy to get busy with life and convince yourself "not now" when it comes to doing regular relationship inventories. To save you a whole lot of drama it's better to detect when someone sitting at your advisory table isn't a good fit any more earlier on.

If you recall in your Mentally Fit Room, beliefs about yourself are mirrored in all your relationships. If your limiting belief is that you are not worthy enough and it has not been addressed, it will show up in all your significant relationships. For example, if you don't feel worthy this could spill over into the quality of people who surround you. You may find yourself on a committee where another committee member undermines or mistreats you in some way. If deep down you feel unworthy to be there or to contribute in a meaningful way, you may feel your power is being robbed.

When you treat yourself with the utmost respect, like taking care of yourself with healthy food, water, fit breaks, and have realistic expectations of yourself, then others will follow suit. How you choose to treat yourself sets the tone for how others treat you.

> *How you choose to treat yourself sets the tone for how others treat you.*

Think of a time when you were unhappy at work, when you felt frustrated, or unappreciated. What were you feeling about yourself at that time? Everyone comes as a teacher. You get to decide whether you want to pass this lesson and move on or continue to repeat the pattern of pain. Life has a way of repeating the lesson until we are ready to get it.

When I stayed in that toxic work environment I shared earlier, I clearly didn't feel I was worthy. If I had, I would have said, "The way I am being treated here is non-negotiable. I am worthy to be treated much better." An 8 doesn't attract a 2 was a phrase I used to say to clients when they attracted unhealthy intimate relationships into their lives. I believe the same is true for our working relationships. What we permit, we promote.

Being a leader means you have to be "on" all the time. Having those safe, trusting, honest, and authentic people who surround you with love, kindness, and truth will help you through this.

Participating in a mastermind group is a fabulous way to get inspired, supported, and help you stretch yourself both professionally and personally.

If you aren't familiar with a mastermind group, they typically have a minimum of four people and a maximum of six. You'll need to research the different goals and formats for a mastermind to find one to best serve your purpose. Ideally you have regular meetings either in person or by video chat. The format is decided by the group.

In one of the masterminds that I participate, we each get 20 minutes to share what is new and good, what challenge or opportunity we are working on, and whether we need feedback or problem solving. It continues to be a game changer for me. These inspiring women are achieving amazing goals and stretching themselves in order to get there. When I hear their successes and their courage to go for it, I am inspired to pursue my dreams in ways I hadn't even thought of. We really are the company we keep.

Human nature is to follow the flock. What if the flock you are surrounding yourself with are people who are stuck in negativity and blaming others for why they are unhappy? It's easy to blame the system, blame the government, blame the clients, blame your entitled employee, but this keeps you a victim or a martyr. You don't own your power when you blame others. The only way to maintain being that powerhouse leader is to surround yourself with like-minded powerhouse leaders. No excuses. No complaining. No blaming others for why you aren't getting the results you want.

When you are with this calibre of thought leaders the focus is on finding the way to get the results you want. There is no place for scarcity thinking. We know the benefits of that trusted friend or colleague who nudges you out the door to take time off or to treat yourself to that book or pedicure you haven't made time for.

The biggest fan at your advisory table needs to be you.

During a mastermind group one of my friends and colleagues shared how exhausted she was with pouring herself into a special project. After our meeting I sent her a photo of me holding a note (see Figure 4) up to remind her to be kind to herself and that I supported and celebrated her hard work and efforts.

Figure 4: **Permission Slip**

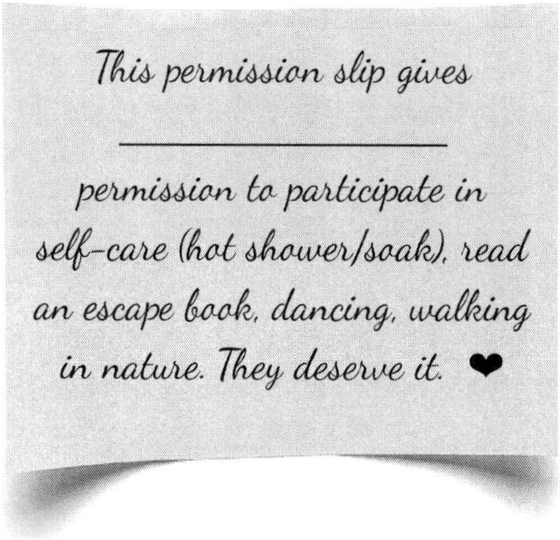

> *This permission slip gives*
> _____
> *permission to participate in self-care (hot shower/soak), read an escape book, dancing, walking in nature. They deserve it.* ♥

Ever find the advice you give someone else is so bang on that you realize you are so passionate about it that you do it for yourself?

Having safe, high-performance thought leaders around you helps you to stay in the power of who you are. They remind you of your strengths, talents, courage, and your purpose of why you are here. They also help you brush yourself off when you make a mistake or hold up a mirror when you are not taking responsibly for something.

You deserve this support, guidance, mutual exchange, and you especially deserve the unconditional love.

My licence plate holder on my car reproduces a quote from Shakespeare, "To thine own self be true."[18] Every time I see this frame, it reminds me to be true to myself. Participating in my powerhouse mastermind groups fast tracks my success, gets me out of self-doubt, and reminds me to dream bigger. When one of my colleagues or friends are playing full out it gives me permission to do the same.

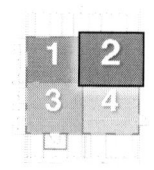

Chapter 10

Love Yourself Now, Not When

To sum up my advice over my past 38 years of helping people remember the power of who they are, I would say make it a lifelong commitment to discover who you are. Make the relationship with yourself one of your most important relationships because how you treat yourself will be the blueprint for how others treat you. There will be times when you have to dig deep to find the root cause of why you feel or do as you do. Do it! The payoff will be worth it. And you are worth it!

Choose Love

My chiropractor, Dr. Mike Coulas from Awakened Life Chiropractic and Wellness Centre, says to ask yourself this question daily, "What would I choose if I loved myself in this situation? Isn't that powerful? Talk about cutting right through any confusion of what to do or not do. When you love yourself, you become more authentic in your decisions, in how you choose to interact, in how you choose to feel, and in how you choose to show up. The next time when someone asks you to sit on a committee, fill in for them, take on yet another commitment, do a favour, trouble-shoot their problems again, ask yourself, "What would I choose if I loved myself right now?"

What would I choose if I loved myself right now?

Tap into the great wisdom within you. For more powerful exercises and solutions for your Emotionally Fit Room, visit my website: https://powerfuljourney.com/emotionallyfitroom

In the Course of Miracles student workbook,[19] the belief is that there are only two feelings – love or a call to love.

Think about one of your staff or a client who acted out in a hurtful way to you or another colleague. Would you agree that in that moment or situation they weren't loving themselves? In that situation their fear, worry, or hurt lashed out at others when the deeper issue is that they were calling out to be loved.

Granted there are times in your workplace where your superior or the stakeholders request something, and you have to act. You still get to choose how you will love yourself during this situation. For example, ask yourself how many hours realistically will this report take? What can I defer until after the report is completed (that doesn't mean cancelling your walk at lunch)? How will I love myself through this deadline?

If I enter each of my Four Rooms every day – Mentally Fit Room, Emotionally Fit Room, Physically Fit Room and Spiritually Fit Room – what actions steps will I take? Start your day with yoga stretches while connecting to your breath to quiet your mind and release your stress, meditate to help with emotional balance, prepare healthy lunches or dinners on Sunday to get ready for the full week, and build in some sharing and connection time with a friend or colleague or family member who brings out the best in you.

I celebrate leaders who create a healthy culture (especially during crunch time for a deadline) where their employees are encouraged to bring in healthy food to share and connect with each other as opposed to sugary treats, donuts, and fast food. The sugar crash and emotional beating up that can follow for many is counterproductive. During emotional times it's natural to reach for comfort foods like pasta, breads, cookies, etc., however if that becomes a habit it negatively impacts you in all four of your Rooms. We will explore creative ways to check into your Physically Fit Room to support your Mental, Emotional, and Spiritual well-being in the next Room.

Loving yourself requires effort and repetition. It's no different than going to the gym and lifting weights. You can't lift 200 pounds on your first day, but with practice, effort, and commitment everything is possible. Before you know it, this "loving yourself muscle" will be so strong that it will be automatic for you to make healthier choices.

As a leader your days are swamped with many demands that deplete your energy. And you don't leave your leadership role at work. You are a leader with your immediate family, likely your extended family, your friends, your church, and your community as a whole. Loving yourself means letting go sometimes. It's important to hang up your wonder woman or superman suit once in a while. You deserve to get filled up. You deserve to step off that stress treadmill to take a breath to just "be", and rest your body, mind, and spirit. Balancing your time between work, play, spirituality, exercise, and relationships is an art. Some days you master it well and others you suck at it. When you don't love yourself your shortcomings often make an appearance. That judgmental part is in each of us, the over-sensitive, self-sabotaging, self-centered, fear-driven, or resentful part.

The Triple-A Method

I use the Triple-A Method: Acknowledge, Accept and take Action.

When your shortcomings surface, *acknowledge* them for the wounded parts of who you are. There is no greater time to work on loving yourself than when you are embarrassed or feel bad about yourself for making a mistake or when you're insecure, sad, hurt, or angry side brought out the worst in you. At some point in your life an experience occurred that helped shape you and this shortcoming was born to help you survive. Ideally remove yourself from the situation. Take a walk, go for a drive, or sit quietly somewhere and be with this awareness of the shortcoming. Let's say it's being judgemental. Ask yourself, "What would I choose in this moment if I loved myself?" First you'd remind yourself that you are a good person who has flaws much like everyone else.

Now that you have acknowledged this you can shift to *accepting* that this is part of being human. And with this new-found knowledge you are able to be kind to yourself for seeing who you really are. Human. Being aware that you were judgemental in a situation frees you up to make better choices in the future. Remember, during the times when you neglect your needs, like getting eight hours of sleep, eating healthy, and exercising, your shortcomings are more likely to show up.

Now you know this shortcoming is present you can take *action* to make changes to be the best version of yourself. Pause before speaking. Ask yourself, "Is what I am about to say inspiring or necessary?" Every change begins with a decision. Committing to a plan means you get to connect, learn, and grow with yourself in a deeper way. The biggest gift you can give yourself is to grow into the person you want to be. Be gentle with yourself as you make these changes. Self-awareness is essential in order to be that powerhouse leader. It's in the self-honesty where hope lies. You are worth this investment.

My wish for you is that you invest in yourself in this way. Make your Emotionally Fit Room a priority and check in daily.

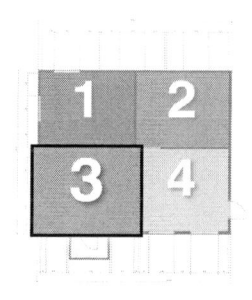

Room Three

YOUR PHYSICALLY FIT ROOM

Partnering with your body so you can operate from that powerhouse place allows you to make clear, concise, and confident choices. Clarity, focus, and added energy are just some of the perks when you treat your body well. Most people walk around feeling tired, unfocused, and overwhelmed. I wonder if there is a connection to what they eat or what they need to eat to support their optimum health? There are reasons athletes don't sit around eating donuts, processed food, and potato chips. They need their minds to be sharp, their bodies to be fast and efficient, and their emotions to be in check.

When you fast forward to the benefits of moving your body, we know that you breathe more deeply, sleep better, have toned muscles and skin, perform at peak mental capacity, experience improved sex drive, and peace of mind washes over your spirit allowing your body to operate at its optimum. You are able to let go more readily, your priorities and what's important become clear. Your ability to not sweat the small stuff increases. You are able to detach with love from the world around you. You are calm and confident. Talk about an all-inclusive.

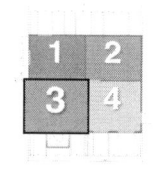

Chapter 11

What Is Your Body Trying to Tell You?

Gloria was a seasoned manager of a social service organization. We would see each other at training events, conferences, and work meetings. I hadn't seen her in several months and was taken back by how exhausted, withdrawn, and pale she looked at this meeting. She shared that her health had declined greatly and she recently had been diagnosed with fibromyalgia. Looking back, she said there were many signs, but she pushed through and ignored the head and body aches, the fatigue, and the lack of energy. Rather than cut back on work hours to rest and reset herself, she forged ahead. Ironically, she said, "My health has deteriorated so much that I have no choice but to step off the ridiculous number of committees I sit on."

The choices you make today determine how you choose to die. Ouch, right?

My hunch is that you don't plan on being hooked up to machines with your family stricken with grief for the pain you are in. Focus on how you want to die and work backwards. I plan to live to 102 and simply drift off to sleep in my own home and not wake up. I will have taught a Pilate's class that morning and then volunteered at a school for troubled kids along with feeling grateful for the recent family visits with our children and grandchildren.

Tap into the great wisdom within you. For more powerful exercises and solutions for your Physically Fit Room, visit my website: https://powerfuljourney.com/physicallyfitroom

What healthy age would you like to live to? Notice I said *healthy* age. It's the quality of life versus the number of years. This is a good opportunity to reflect on what is working in your current lifestyle and what doesn't work.

Get to Know Your Body

Listening to what your body is trying to tell you is important for your overall well-being.

When you remember that you are 100% responsible for nourishing your body with healthy foods, getting eight hours of sleep, and taking exercise breaks, you will build your immune system. Regardless of who is sick around you this healthy lifestyle will protect you from the ongoing stress, allow you to bounce back from an injury, and give you that much needed energy to perform at your best.

Like any relationship, it takes time to get to know someone. It is the same with your body. Once you stay alert and aware to your body's cues of discomfort, pain, and joy, you will be equipped with valuable knowledge of how to act accordingly. A great book by Gabor Maté[20] explores the role of the mind-body link in conditions and diseases such as arthritis, cancer, diabetes, heart disease, Irritable Bowel Syndrome, and multiple sclerosis. I am not celiac, however my body thanks me when I avoid white and whole wheat flour and minimize the amount of dairy in my diet.

A Powerhouse Body

Why would your relationship with your body matter when it comes to you being a powerhouse leader? Easy. Your body is intertwined with your mind, emotions, and spirit. They all work together, in harmony. When you treat your body like a jaguar it will operate like the genius and superior being that you are. When you weigh your body down with unhealthy foods like processed sugar, work into the wee hours to meet a deadline, or avoid moving your body, you are not operating at your full potential.

Most people use their body more like a pleasure centre rather than seeing it as sacred and in need of nourishment. We eat fast, we talk fast, and we keep busy. Food has become a way to numb our discomfort and anxiety, which in turn can cause guilt and shame. This has resulted in the rise in food addiction causing obesity and physical and mental health issues. The media's influence on how our bodies should look reinforces the message that your body is not quite good enough. And the cycle continues.

A cultural shift is needed to embrace our bodies with respect, love, and kindness.

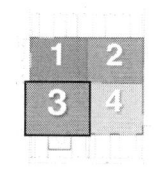

Chapter 12

How Are You Self-Protecting While Under Stress?

We all experience stress in our daily lives to varying degrees, and it seems to be on the rise. Some stress helps us feel alive and excited about our life. Our pulse speeds up and our hormones surge, but there is no threat or fear. This kind of stress contributes to our lives in positive ways. We feel this type of stress when we ride a roller coaster, compete for a promotion, meet a deadline, or get ready for a vacation. It helps us accomplish tasks efficiently and boosts our memory.

Long-term stress, on the other hand, can be harmful. When stress becomes overwhelming and drawn out, the risks for mental health problems like anxiety, depression, substance abuse, sleep problems, headaches, and the likelihood of medical problems increase.

The Physical Effects of Stress

Knowing how stress effects your body is important. How you respond physically will give you a framework to work with.

You've likely heard about the "flight or fight" response, also known as your stress response. It includes both physical and mental responses to your perception of different situations. This stress response is your body's way of protecting you. That same hard wiring that protected the caveman

---

Tap into the great wisdom within you. For more powerful exercises and solutions for your Physically Fit Room, visit my website: https://powerfuljourney.com/physicallyfitroom

against predators and other threats lies within you. Your body doesn't know the difference from a wild charging beast or a looming deadline. When your stress response gets activated, your body releases substances like adrenaline and cortisol.

Cortisol is your main stress hormone and it increases glucose (sugars) in your bloodstream, heightens your brain's use of glucose, and amplifies the accessibility of substances that repair tissues. Cortisol also limits functions that would be unnecessary or damaging in a fight or flight situation, such as digestion.

There are two main ways of coping with stress: hypo-arousal and hyper-arousal.

Arousal pertains to the physiological state of preparedness or general state of excitement of your nervous system. Your arousal state lies on a continuum from low to high, coupled with the ability to maintain ideal arousal levels is often required for adaptive interaction with your environment.

Hypo-arousal refers to an arousal state that sits at the low end of the scale. When observing someone who is experiencing hypo-arousal, they may respond under-responsive to stimuli in their environment. Some examples include apathy, lack of focus, lethargy, or boredom.

On the other end of the spectrum there is emotional hyper-arousal which may appear as extreme emotions, sleeping problems, difficulties concentrating, irritability, and angry outbursts. Someone with emotional hyper-arousal may have passionate thoughts, reactions, and feelings that are more intense than the average person.

> Hyperarousal is a primary symptom of post-traumatic stress disorder (PTSD). It occurs when a person's body suddenly kicks into high alert as a result of thinking about their trauma. Even though real danger may not be present, their body acts as if it is, causing lasting stress after a traumatic event.
>
> PTSD can affect people of any age, including children.[21]

On average people who practice meditation regularly have lower cortisol levels than those who don't, according to a study from the University of Lausanne.[22] For instance, practicing yoga helps calm your breathing and this appears to be linked to a reduction in cortisol levels. Other great ways to release your stress include engaging in relaxing outlets like your favourite hobby, such as knitting, reading, gardening, or baking.

Tuning in to how your body responds to stress will help.
- Do you tend to get headaches if you have been working at your computer for long periods of time?
- Does your stomach ache or feel off?
- How about your back, does it hurt?
- Do you get a pain in the neck?
- Do you have a racing mind that disrupts your sleep?

Stress Behaviours

Each one of us reacts differently. Having the awareness of how you self-protect will serve you well (see Exercise 12). It all starts with a thought. Think about how you responded during a recent crisis or tragedy, COVID-19 for example. Did you jump into action, did you become paralyzed with fear, did you find yourself over-reacting to simple situations, were you patient or impatient, did you pour all of yourself into your teams and organization leaving yourself depleted for the people that matter most?

There is no judgement here, only observation, but the outcome is the same: disconnection from yourself, your team, and your goals. Fear becomes the dominant driver. Fear of what you might lose, fear of being exposed, fear of being blamed, fear of being judged, fear of not being liked and the list goes on.

When a traumatic event is occurring, there is a heightened sensitivity to those around us resulting in people taking things more personally. The risk of triggering each other's insecurities becomes greater. Once you become aware of your coping style, you will be more sensitive to the coping styles of others. Behaviour does have a purpose.

Sharing the self-protection list (Exercise 12) at a team meeting will be a great self-awareness and team-building exercise. Pay attention to the next time a team member becomes needy and wants your approval on every decision they make, or if another is intolerant of their own mistakes or the mistakes of others or blames or gossips about colleagues. Each of their responses is a reflection of their inner world where fear and insecurity reside. Having a safe and open environment will nurture this invaluable self-awareness and feedback to help each other take more health breaks, mental health days, vacations, and bring their best selves to the table when under stress.

Exercise 12

IDENTIFYING YOUR SELF-PROTECTION BEHAVIOUR

This self-protection list comes from my observations and interactions with my clients coupled with workshops, books, and the great mentorship I have experienced. As we talk, it becomes very clear to them when they slip into self-protection mode. They know if they don't replace their current behaviours with healthier responses, their emotions can destroy their intelligence. I am confident this self-protection list will help you identify which behaviour you commonly exhibit while under stress.

Step 1
Circle your most common response from the list below.

- **Domination:** Taking over and dominating the situation. Focus is on doing things my way versus being open to your team's ideas.
- **Intellectualizing:** Talking quickly with emphasis on theories.
- **Sarcasm:** Using humour or sarcasm at inappropriate times.
- **Blaming Others:** Focusing on being right or avoiding joint responsibility.
- **Gossiping:** Talking inappropriately about team members behind their backs.
- **Ostrich in the Sand:** Denying or avoiding the situation and not addressing the issues; working excessive hours to avoid feeling your fear.
- **Playing Victim:** Focusing on being powerless and having no choices. This includes second-guessing your actions. "I'm too confused on what to do. I am not smart enough or I am not good enough."
- **Being Political:** Saying what you think people want to hear.
- **Negativity:** Focusing on the problem and how hard it is. Perfectionism may arise
- **Procrastinating:** Leaving things to the last minute and causing yourself undue stress.
- **Withdrawing:** Isolating yourself.

Step 2
Write your circled self-protection behaviour here.

Now that you've ascertained your go-to reaction when under stress, let's replace it with a healthier, more productive option. If withdrawing or isolating is your self-protective response, create a plan to course correct by becoming aware and taking different action while under stress. Use that powerful statement, "What would I choose now if I truly loved myself?"

▶ Example

Instead of isolating, I will:

1. Build in monthly supervision or mentor meetings to share and get feedback on how my leadership experience might serve me.
2. Commit to a communication college or university course to provide some insight.
3. Consistently connect, informally or formally, with other liked-minded leaders to supply open exchanges.
4. Create or join a mastermind group or work with an accountability partner to keep myself connected and supported.

Now it's your turn. "What would I choose instead, if I truly loved myself?

Instead of _____ (your self-protection behaviour here), I will:

_____

_____

_____

_____

Ask your selected support person (assistant, trusted colleague, family member) what they observe your response to be during stressful times. It may be the same or it may be different. Knowledge is power.

Good for you for identifying what your "go-to" self-protective response is. Awareness leads the way to growth and change.

Step 3

Give permission to your selected support people to bring to your attention when you slip into self-protection mode. They might say, "You don't seem like yourself. Is everything okay? I noticed you are more upset or withdrawn. How can I best support you right now?"

Armed with the awareness of how you self-protect will provide you with much needed feedback.

Armed with the awareness of how you self-protect will provide you with much needed feedback on when to step off the stress treadmill to do self-care or self-compassion in order to bring out the best in you. Checking into your Four Rooms daily will help you identify when you have slipped into past unhealthy behaviours and how to interrupt that pattern by replacing it with healthier coping strategies.

Feeding Your Stress

Let's come right out of the gate with the truth about our society.

Research out of Memorial University estimated that by 2019 most (55.4%) of the Canadian adult population will be categorized as overweight (34.2%) or obese (21.2%).[23] According to a new study led by Harvard T.H. Chan School of Public Health, "The study's researchers estimate that, currently, 40% of American adults have obesity and 18% have severe obesity."[24] Additionally, a Position Statement from the Heart and Stroke Foundation Canada states, "Overweight and obesity contribute to type 2 diabetes, high blood pressure and some cancers and are a risk factor for heart disease and stroke."[25]

Why is it our society is more overweight than ever before? I realize there are many factors however I would like you to consider this. Might it be that these diets and extreme fasting methods don't work? What if your body is actually supporting you instead of turning on you when it gains weight? What if it is insulating you from either your external world or your internal world, or both? The reason for your weight gain is the need to protect yourself from whatever is going on in your life. Is your limiting belief of "not feeling you're good enough" showing up? What fears are you stuffing down? Do you need to do a better job at saying "no" more? Do you rarely give yourself permission to get angry?

I know for me, the times I gain weight are during times I am not owning my power. It can be as simple as getting off the phone with a family member who is stressed out again, which results in me feeling depleted, anxious, or frustrated. Reaching into the fridge is my way to numb or stuff down how powerless I felt. What would your negative self-talk look like? "You checked yourself outside the conversation again and pretended that your feelings, your thoughts, or your life didn't matter."

Sometimes the weight gain is protecting you from yourself. What you permit, you promote. Getting caught up in this unhealthy pattern can erode your self-esteem and make you question whether you do matter or whether you've abandoned yourself again by not speaking up. The relationship with yourself is the most important relationship you will ever experience. Consistently carving out time in your schedule to get to know your likes, your dislikes, what brings your body joy, what makes your body feel confident, and tuning in to your body's cues when it needs more self-care helps. Being kind to yourself along this journey will be important.

> *Being kind to yourself along this journey will be important.*

Writing this book took me out of my comfort zone. I experienced fear and second guessed myself because I didn't know what I didn't know. In order to minimize the intensity of my negative self-talk, I knew I needed to avoid weighing my body and my mind down with unhealthy foods. Intuitively, it made sense for me to do everything I possibly could to keep my body, mind, and spirit as clear and healthy as possible so I could step into my power fully. I knew from past experience that when I ate clean, I operated from a clear, confident, and no-nonsense place. It's like I tap into my higher self where the inner wisdom lives. I made the commitment to eat vegetarian Monday through Friday with no processed sugar or gluten. I gave myself permission to enjoy myself on the weekend within moderation. What health habits have you used to keep your body, mind, and spirit at their optimum health to complete a deadline, union negotiations, or during a time when you needed to "be on?"

Teaching fitness and being immersed in the health and wellness field for the past 30 years has taught me so much. We are all different shapes and sizes. Regardless of your size at this moment, when you love and accept yourself fully and completely now, not when you lose the weight, the weight will fall off. Too easy, right? Actually, it is. Accepting your body shape as it is matters. If your body type is a size 14 and you spend your life trying to make it a size 7, you are in for a roller coaster ride. I don't know about you, but I am beyond tired of trying to make my body something that it isn't meant to be.

Moving Your Stress

When you are at your optimal health you have more energy, more focus, sleep better, have fewer or no sugar cravings, have razor sharp clarity, make healthier decisions, have clear boundaries, and are confident. Being aware and taking action when your food triggers, stress triggers, and your limiting beliefs show up is important. Being a powerhouse leader requires effort, consistency, self-compassion, self-love, and acceptance along with maintaining this meaningful relationship with yourself. Treat yourself as if you matter. Because you most certainly do matter.

One leader shared that the first thing to go when she has deadlines, changes in her organization, or family challenges is her fitness program or routine. Mentally she knows it is the very thing she needs during that stressful time, but she has exhausted herself so much that she convinces herself she doesn't have time or that someone in her life (staff, family, friend, pet) has more important needs than going for a walk, the gym, yoga, etc. Amazing how we push away the very thing we need most.

Often you know what you don't like, however it is important to explore what you do like. Perhaps you dislike running but enjoy yoga or walking. Maybe you dislike spin classes (okay, that's me), but working out in a group setting at a gym or one-on-one with a trainer is your thing. The options are endless. Get out that detective magnifying glass and research what you realistically want for your body to experience. Talk with other people within your circle about their interests and their hobbies related to moving your body.

So, what is your fitness goal? Maybe it's to hike in a certain area, ride your bike from one city to another, take a fitness class that normally would scare you off, become a yoga or Pilates instructor, take a meditation class, take a dance class, or any number of things. Schedule in dates and times with yourself to get to know yourself and what matters most.

Let's say you picked Wednesday night or Saturday morning to be for you. Keep a running list of all the things that spark your interest and write them down. Stay in possibility thinking versus analyzing why it isn't a good idea. You could even buy a beautiful journal for yourself and keep all your dreams and desires in there. Hiking a mountain may be a deep desire. Give yourself permission to say, "Why not me?" As you create your fitness list be flexible and let it evolve. Keep an open mind to trying different activities.

As a fearless leader, your days are filled from the moment you wake up to when you go to sleep. If exercise is not currently part of your routine it may seem impossible to find a place in your schedule. The starting point is believing you deserve to take care of your body in order to be more focused, more effective, calmer, and make better decisions.

Think of someone at your workplace who goes for a walk or takes in a fitness class before work or during their lunch break. What do you notice about them? They are energized, upbeat, positive, and calm. There is a lightness to their step. They are enjoyable to be around.

When sitting in front of your computer for hours, it's easy to forget that sitting in one position and using the same muscles is much like working in a factory and doing something repetitively. "Sitting is the new smoking" is becoming a common refrain. Getting up every hour is important to shift your body and your energy. Exercise 13 provides a few stretching exercises that will help.

Exercise 13

STRETCHING

This stretch is fabulous for releasing tension in your neck.
> Pull your chair away from your desk. Sit on the edge of the chair.
> Place your left hand behind your head and touch your right ear.
> Allow your right arm and hand to gently reach towards the floor.
> Hold the stretch for a minimum of 10 seconds. Then switch sides.

Brain gym is an effective program that is worthy of learning about. Dr. Paul E. Dennison and Gail Dennison were educators who created Brain Gym[26] in the early 1970s. Brain Gym® uses movements to fast-track learning and enhance performance. This is performed through sets of exercises that connect the left side of your brain with the right side. It helps you focus and be more grounded. Try Exercise 14.

If you have gotten out of the routine of moving your body, how about you start small. Each day move your body for 20 minutes. You can organically decide the morning of, or you can strategically schedule time into your day. Knowing when you are more likely to exercise during the day is important. Setting yourself up for success is key. When I am presenting my training or keynotes, I make sure the morning of the event I am in the gym. If you know you have a big meeting or event that you are feeling a bit anxious or nervous about build in exercise time prior. You will be refreshed and on point for your event.

Exercise 14

BRAIN GYM EXERCISE

You can do this Brain Gym exercise standing or sitting.

First, reach or touch your opposite elbow to your opposite knee. Do this about 8 times.

Then raise your arms shoulder height with your hands facing each other. Cross one wrist over the other and clasp your palms together. Scoop your clasped hands and let them touch your heart. Cross your ankles. Take your tongue to the roof of your mouth and keep it there. Take three deep breaths by breathing in through your nose and out through your nose. Once completed, shake out your arms and legs.

Pause for a moment. Notice how you feel in your body. Feel the peace. Feel the grounding. This exercise will not only help you focus more but it will bring you back to the present moment.

Protecting Your Heart

Releasing the stress from your body is not something to take lightly. Women have now caught up to men when it comes to having a heart attack.[27]

I have never liked the term heart attack because the heart does not attack you. It is what you do to the heart that it becomes attacked. If you listen long enough to someone sharing about a relative or friend who has had a heart attack, you will find the answer. They were overweight, they were a workaholic, they were intense, they overindulged in alcohol, they didn't eat well, and the list goes on. My point is that life is not meant to be overindulging in anything for long periods of time.

I had a friend some years ago say that his heart attack was the best thing that ever happened to him. He had put status, prestige, pride, and ego in front of everything. He had protected his heart by not sharing openly with the people he cared for the most about how he felt. After, he sat down with each of his children and his spouse and shared from his heart how much they meant to him. There were many tears and hugs as you can imagine. He let his heart attack be a wakeup call for the underlying issues in his life.

According to the Heart and Stroke Foundation of Canada:

> The most common heart attack sign is chest pain or discomfort; however, women can experience a heart attack without chest pressure. They may experience shortness of breath, pressure or pain in the lower chest or upper abdomen, dizziness, light-headedness or fainting, upper back pressure or extreme fatigue.[28]

One of my keynote addresses is entitled, "Is Your Leadership Underwear Too Tight? Learn the Letting Go Formula." When you are all wound up, you miss out on truly connecting with joy, peace of mind, and gratitude. Standing in your power as a leader requires energy. If there is no energy to be found because you are overcommitting yourself, you will experience mental, physical, and emotional fatigue. Creating and maintaining healthy habits allows you to show up as the best version of yourself.

Your Pain Is a Warning

Pain is often a driver for most of us. Until we hit a wall of discomfort or pain, we don't seem to pay attention to what is right in front of us.

When we don't get the lesson, life has a way of coming around again and helping us experience it.

Sadly, I have observed some leaders experience very traumatic physical pain and completely miss the boat on the connection to their body, mind, and spirit (see Exercise 15). Their pain is simply a warning that they need to pay attention or something worse will happen. Their body is telling them something is out of alignment. Convinced it is strictly a physical issue, they run from one doctor and specialist's appointment to another with minimal or no pain relief. Others get a second chance at life by having a successful surgery to remove the cancer or tumor, only to return to the rat race they just came out of or to situations where their voice is stifled or absent. When we don't get the lesson, life has a way of coming around again and helping us experience it. Eventually, we run out of chances.

Exercise 15

CHECK IN WITH YOUR BODY

Check in with your body now.
>What does it need from you?
>- Rest. Create a technology-free zone in your bedroom to get the much needed eight hours of sleep.
>- Reduce sugar or caffeine.
>- Reduce your alcohol intake.
>- Recharge your body by moving your body daily.

Mother Nature as a Healer

We all know the power of connecting with Mother Nature to help release stress. So get outside, rake leaves, garden, run, bike, sit by the water, and any other activities. Mother Nature has been waiting for you. She has this peaceful way of grounding you if only for five minutes. Daily doses of Mother Nature have an instant impact on your spirit.

I remind my clients to remove their shoes and feel their feet on the grass and do some deep breathing. Take a walk by yourself or with a family member. That simple act of walking away from your responsibilities and all the deadlines breathes new life back into you. Your life will be more manageable when you return. Mother Nature connects me with my humanness. I realize some of you may be removed from nature due to the location of your office. Why not bring nature to you? A soothing desk fountain, plants (live not fake), decorate with rocks if you like them, or consider paintings that reflect nature. Investing the time in creating a calm and relaxed work environment will help soothe you. This doesn't replace your lunchtime or after work walks or work outs, of course, but it will provide you with a much-welcomed Mother Nature connection.

Working with leaders and teams in a retreat setting is my sweet spot. I get to observe these amazing people pause and reflect on who they are, who they are yet to be, and feel the power of connecting with other leaders or team members in a way that their offices or meeting rooms do not allow. Mother Nature holds the space for them to relax and let go of all their pressures and the daily grind of life. The insights, aha moments, increased self-compassion, and connection is visible.

When I work with leaders who get the value of supporting their team in a retreat, the gratitude and growth from their team is massive. Some team members would never have the financial or physical opportunity to attend a retreat, so this employee investment elicits trust, loyalty, respect, and resilience that impacts your whole organization. When you invest in your team in this way, you invest in your organization's optimum results. Your people can only give of their talent, their energy and their skills for so long before burning out sets in. When leaders build in this resilient plan of action, like a team retreat or training, it prevents damage control later. You experience fewer sick leaves, less mental health issues, less conflict, less gossip, less turn over, and more connected, loyal, and resilient team members. According to a CAMH report in 2020 mental illness is a leading cause of disability in Canada. Some of their findings included that every week at least 500,000 Canadians miss work due to mental illness resulting in devastating impacts to them personally, their workplace, and to our economy. Roughly $51 billion is spent annually because of the burden of mental illness resulting in lost productivity of $6.3 billion.[29]

I know what burn out feels like – a constant state of anxiety, fearfulness, a feeling of being overwhelmed, and exhaustion, among other things. For me I attend two retreats per year to invest in my leadership journey both as a facilitator and as a human being. I believe that great leaders allow themselves to be students.

We don't know what we don't know. However, when you make it a habit to listen to the signals from your body you will have prevented many illnesses and pain from graduating to the next level or prevent them from ever existing. It is never too late. Wherever you are right now with your body's well-being and fitness level is exactly where you are supposed to be. Shifting to a better way of being and thinking all starts with a decision to be better.

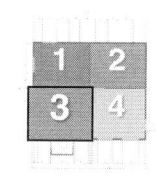

Chapter 13

Nourishing Your Body with Healthy Foods

Learning to listen to your body's cues is essential. What does this have to do with you being a powerhouse leader? Your Physically Fit Room needs to be in top shape to navigate all the fires you put out, all the decisions you need to make, all the different personalities you need to engage and work with, and in order to perform at your best. What you eat and when you eat matters. I know of people who don't eat their first meal of the day until 2 or 3 p.m., others who swear by eating breakfast to start their day, and others who have small meals throughout the day. Personally, I think you need to discover for yourself what works best for you. Pay attention to the feedback from your body. It will guide you. I like routine when it comes to eating.

Listen to Your Body

I like to keep my life simple. In my early fitness training, I learned to focus on making sure my output is greater than my input. In other words, if I know I am going to have a large meal I need to be prepared to move my body after. I am sure you have all sorts of tricks up your sleeve when it comes to pacing your food intake, like drinking water before your meal, filling up on the vegetables, avoiding or having a small dessert.

Tap into the great wisdom within you. For more powerful exercises and solutions for your Physically Fit Room, visit my website: https://powerfuljourney.com/physicallyfitroom

Not having certain treats in the house helps me. If it isn't accessible to me, I won't eat it. Food prep and planning a week ahead, rethinking how I will reward myself after a project or stressful time, and minimizing going to buffets works for me. Instead of food being my reward, I treat myself to a good book, hot soak, calling a friend, or a healthy meal. I wish I could tell you I am 100% faithful to doing this, however that would be a lie. I am a work in progress. Progress not perfection. When I stick to the plan my body thanks me with calmness, confidence, and peace of mind. To discover your body's relationship with food, check out Exercise 16.

Exercise 16
WHAT FOOD FITS YOUR BODY?

What foods do not agree with your body?

_____

_____

Does your body tell you through bloating, cramping, constipation, or aches and pains that its best if you avoid that food?

_____

Do you have a love-hate relationship with a particular food?

_____

_____

Do you play games with yourself and try to talk yourself into eating something that you know your body has already shown doesn't work for you?

_____

_____

Make a list of the best "cheat" foods that work for you when you are tired, putting in long hours, and need self-compassion.

"Cheat" Foods that Work (favourite fruit, popcorn, yummy dips with vegetables)

_____   _____

_____   _____

_____   _____

Make a list of the tempting foods – your traditional go-to foods – that make you suffer later.

"Cheat" Foods that Don't Work (chips, ice cream, sugar treats)

_____   _____

_____   _____

_____   _____

Keep the first list ("Cheat" Foods that Work) in a prominent place (on your fridge) so they become your go-to foods. If you do give into temptation allow yourself a do-over – or a reset or clean slate.

Forgive yourself for not treating yourself with the utmost respect it deserves and move on. Focus your attention on the reset and what your next right choice is. Jump into action by cutting up loads of vegetables and commit to detoxing your body with hot water and lemon and make sure your choices today will be healthier. Too often we can stay stuck in emotionally beating ourselves up causing ourselves more pain. Let it go. You are human. Refer back to the question, "What would I choose to eat if I loved myself?

Body Image

You are beautiful, just the way you are – not when you lose weight, not when you get a nose job, not when you get your teeth fixed, not when you buy special facial cream that makes you look five years younger, not when you finally measure up to your partner or friend. Weight loss, diets, and body image have been a dominant part of every girl and woman's life (see Exercise 17). I have had the privilege to work with some very high achievers and obsession with body image is a common theme among female leaders. As shared above, between our fast-paced society and very high standards, the negative impact of stress on your body compounds over time. You might be wondering how body image even has a place in this book. Powerhouse leadership from the inside out includes how you perceive your mind, body, and spirit. If gaining or losing weight is a concern for you these questions will help you overcome that inner nagging that holds you back from fully experiencing your successes and accepting yourself now, not when.

Exercise 17
REFLECTIONS OF BODY IMAGE

Take some time to consider the messages you received as a child about your body. Here are some questions that will help you reflect.

1. What was the common theme within your family about your body?

2. Was your appearance or weight an important topic? How so? For example, did you feel your body was invisible or was a theme of weight gain or loss talked about a lot?

3. Was it talked about with sarcastic humour? How? What was said?

4. Was your body celebrated? If yes, how? Engage in open or private discussions about taking good care of your body with healthy foods/exercise/touch.

_____

_____

_____

Knowing where some of your body image beliefs come from will help you get clear about how you help your body or harm it with the food choices you make.

A Powerhouse Eating Plan

I want to go back to that game-changing self-reflection question. Ask yourself, "What would I choose in this moment if I loved myself?" For me, this is at the heart of all my decisions today.

Yes, I may choose to treat myself to chocolate or other treats and enjoy it. However, if I am truly loving myself, my body purrs like a jaguar when I eat healthy, life-enhancing foods. Some rock-star superfoods include avocados, beans, broccoli, flaxseed, garlic, salmon, yogurt, kale, spinach, blueberries, and, yippee, 70%+ dark chocolate – I prefer all the veggies and fruits to be organic. There is no official list of superfoods, but this particular list comes from my naturopathic doctor, Dr. Michael Rahman, Pinewood Natural Health Centre.[30] Equally important is to avoid the dirty dozen, if you cannot buy organic. These include blueberries, strawberries, potatoes, kale, spinach, cherry tomatoes, apples, cucumbers, celery, cherries, peaches, and grapes.

Food is our best medicine and our current diet sucks. You have likely heard the phrase, "Eat your food like medicine, otherwise you will need to eat your medicine as food." The North American diet primarily consists of sugar, sodium, and a number of other chemicals that don't support your gut health. This diet has caused severe inflammation throughout our bodies that is a big contributor to hypertension, diabetes, cancer, arthritis, and the list goes on.

What you put in your mouth either helps or hurts your body.

We are a sugar addicted society. I see it much like alcohol or tobacco use. Once it enters your system the craving and addiction kicks in. And that one piece of licorice or that one cookie won't cut it. You need more to feed the sugar gremlin. We all play games with ourselves when it comes to food. For all the time spent on negotiating when and how much you will enjoy something we could have cured a disease by now.

Diane is a successful CEO, who I work with. I admire how disciplined she is with her eating habits. She brings a packed lunch to work consisting of loads of vegetables, homemade dip, protein, and other high energy snacks. Her staff eat out most days and comment on how she needs to loosen up with her routine. She is confident her eating routine keeps her healthy when they come down with colds or flus and she doesn't. She is a great power of example for her team.

I have also worked with the opposite leader who brings donuts, candies, and chocolate into the office on a regular basis to treat her staff. Sadly, when I worked with her team many of them were unhappy with their weight and were experiencing health issues. As a leader it is important that you take that eagle's eye view of what you and your team need to perform at your very best. Everything within balance of course. Occasional treats are great, however being clear about your overall team culture needs to be a priority.

I have had the honour to work with many dynamic and creative teams over the years and their commitment to health was inspiring to me. Some teams did salad potluck Fridays, others shared healthy recipes, and others set up walking groups, informally or formally.

Naturally, you want to have more energy, more focus, more confidence, and more peace of mind. What you put in your mouth either helps or hurts your body. When buying your food, focus on the top five ingredients in each food purchase so you can make the best choices for you. You will be alarmed at how much sugar and sodium is listed. Through my research, candida, or yeast infections, are a common condition in women when you consume a lot of sugar. I wish my family physician had educated me on this.

The Theory Behind Adrenal Fatigue

As long as your world continues to be fast paced and you remain in stress overload, it is important for you to understand how your adrenal glands work to support you. Our adrenal glands are small glands located on top of each kidney. They produce hormones that you can't live without, including sex hormones and cortisol. Cortisol helps you respond to stress and has many other important functions.

Making too much or not enough of these hormones results in adrenal gland disorders. The term "adrenal fatigue" was coined in 1998 by James Wilson, PhD, a naturopath and expert in alternative medicine.[31] He describes it as a "group of related signs and symptoms (a syndrome) that results when the adrenal glands function below the necessary level." He goes on to say that it's usually associated with intense stress and often follows chronic infections, like bronchitis, flu, or pneumonia.

Wilson says people suffering from adrenal fatigue may not have any physical signs of illness but still may feel tired, "grey," and have fatigue that doesn't get better with sleep. They also crave salty snacks.

When your adrenal glands are stretched by eating fast, stress, lack of sleep, and consuming sugar and sodium, it affects you on many levels. You are exhausted, have poor concentration or brain fog, are more irritable and anxious, and your overall health feels off and sluggish. Taking adrenal supplements helps for sure, but slowing down is huge.

Slow down your breath. Slow down how you talk. Slow down when you eat. Slow down your lifestyle. I know you may be thinking, "This all sounds wonderful Cate, however, you don't know my unmanageable schedule." Actually, I do. And on that unrealistic schedule I burned out many years ago. My anxiety was off the charts, my sleep was disrupted from my racing mind, I was lost in a sea of responsibilities and had no idea where to start, until I stepped off the stress treadmill and honestly looked at my life.

The more you focus on your health and well-being, the clearer your decisions will be. It was only when I reset my diet and lifestyle that I became clear on what I needed to let go of and focus on what my primary responsibilities were in order to experience freedom and peace of mind.

Feel free to check out the health and wellness links I have listed on my website (https://powerfuljourney.com/thepowerhouseinyou). I have also included newsletters I receive that have current research and suggestions on how to experience optimum health.

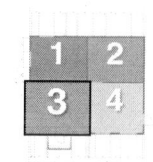

Chapter 14

Your Health Is in the Toilet

Let's talk about your poop for a moment shall we. I have heard it said that your health is in the toilet. This statement comes from the idea that the colour and condition of your bowel movement indicates whether you are healthy or unhealthy. You may need to make only a few adjustments, however consistently observing your bowel movements will act as a preventative measure before anything gets more serious.

Your Bowel Habits

A minimum of one bowel movement per day is a strong indicator of your digestive health.

Michael Cheng, M.D., a Piedmont gastroenterologist, describes a healthy movement.

> Healthy stool is usually considered a soft, formed bowel movement that is typically brownish in color. Changes in the color, shape and texture of your stool can reveal signs of infection, digestive issues or more serious health problems, such as cancer. There is cause for concern when stool is black or reddish, which may be indicative of gastrointestinal bleeding. Stools that are gray in color may also be concerning for liver problems.
>
> And yellow, greasy, foul-smelling stool indicates that the intestines didn't properly digest and absorb fat. This could be

---

Tap into the great wisdom within you. For more powerful exercises and solutions for your Physically Fit Room, visit my website: https://powerfuljourney.com/physicallyfitroom

caused by a disease of the intestinal lining such as celiac disease or chronic pancreatitis.

It's important to maintain good bowel health, as 70 percent of the body's immune system is contained within the digestive tract. To keep your bowel movements frequent and healthy, Dr. Cheng suggests the following tip:

Eat a balanced, high-fiber diet. Fiber can help prevent or relieve constipation. Try fiber-rich foods like apples, carrots, beans, and exercise.[32]

Helping Your Organs

Detoxing as a Reset

Detoxing your body is an important way to reset your organs (especially your liver) and your bowels. You absorb toxins from your work and home environments from chemical cleaners, pesticides, and those scented washroom sprays, candles, or air fresheners. (I'm not a fan of any chemicals in my cleaning products.)

Master Cleanse is a great detox formula that I do at least twice per year. This detox was created by Stanley Burroughs in 1941 with the intent to detoxify the body and for weight loss. My naturopathic doctor recommended I try it. Talking with your doctor or naturopathic doctor will be important before trying anything like this.

> *Before doing a Master Cleanse talking with your doctor or naturopathic doctor is important.*

The Master Cleanse detox consists of using organic lemons, maple syrup, good quality water, and cayenne pepper. Ideally, drinking this mixture from three to ten days allows for any toxins to be cleared from your body. Since I am anemic, eating no food during the day is not an option. When I do this detox, I simply have one main vegetable meal (might be dinner) per day. The increased energy, better sleep, youthful skin, calm spirit, along with feeling clear and focused, keeps me coming back for more. Weight loss occurs too, but the primary reason for this detox is to eliminate toxins from your body and to do a body reset.

There are any number of detox programs you may consider. You may eliminate processed sugar, caffeine, or meat from your diet for 21 days as a form of detoxifying your body. My husband and I try to eat a vegetarian diet through the week and have chicken, fish, or red meat on the weekend.

Regular Exercise

Regular exercise helps prevent constipation and allows you to have regular bowel movements.

The Canadian Physical Activity Guidelines states:[33]

> To achieve health benefits, adults aged 18-64 years should accumulate at least 150 minutes of moderate- to vigorous-intensity aerobic physical activity per week, in bouts of 10 minutes or more. It is also beneficial to add muscle and bone strengthening activities using major muscle groups, at least 2 days per week. More physical activity provides greater health benefits.

Keep Hydrated

Staying hydrated throughout your day also supports moving your bowels along with many other benefits.

There are a few formulas regarding the optimum intake of water. I have heard 8 ounces of water per 25 pounds is recommended and others say eight 8-ounce glasses of water per day is advised. Keep in mind this means plain water, or adding slices of lemon. It does not mean water with flavours or sugar in it.

According to Healthline, staying well hydrated offers a host of health benefits that include higher energy levels and better brain function, just to name a few.[34]

But not all water is created equal, with some being cheaper or providing more nutrients than others. Tap water is contaminated with plastics. We drink reverse osmosis at home.

I believe that knowing who you are and what works for you is important. I too enjoy cookies, baked breads, and treats, however as part of my health regime and to best support my bowels and my overall health, I prefer not to have these items in the house. You see, they call to me from other Rooms, especially when I have not participated in self-care or pushed myself too hard. In other words if it is there, I will eat it. If I go out and enjoy it that seems to work better rather than having the yummy treat in our home.

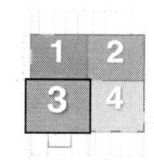

Chapter 15

Sleep Matters

Our lives have become so full with each waking moment that many of us find it difficult to get enough sleep, fall asleep, or stay asleep. There are a variety of factors that may be connected with this crisis of sleep. Exposure to artificial light at night (technology), caffeine consumption, work demands, social commitments, and family dynamics are a few examples that have been identified.

You have likely heard that seven to nine hours of quality sleep per night is important. Your body needs time to restore and repair tissue and integrate your hormones, among other things. Some leaders have tried to convince themselves that less sleep works for them.

Are We Experiencing a Sleep Crisis?

One out of three adults don't get enough sleep according to Centers for Disease Control and Prevention.[35] The negative impacts include obesity, type 2 diabetes, higher incidence of injuries, depression, irritability, and many other side effects. Christopher Barnes, Ph.D., associate professor of management at the University of Washington's Foster School of Business, prepared a review of some interesting research into sleep, or the lack of sleep, and leadership.[36]

Tap into the great wisdom within you. For more powerful exercises and solutions for your Spiritually Fit Room, visit my website: https://powerfuljourney.com//physicallyfitroom

An international study conducted in 2017 by the Center for Creative Leadership found that among leaders, the problem is even worse: 42% get six or fewer hours of shut-eye a night.

In a recent study [2017] Cristiano Guarana and I ... found that sleep-deprived leaders were more impatient, irritable, and antagonistic, which resulted in worse relationships. ... However, the leaders were completely unaware of the negative dynamic.

. . .

When the boss doesn't feel rested, the whole team pays a price.

This lack of sleep in our society is causing us unnecessary problems. I can't help but wonder about the connection between the lack of sleep and over-reactive and unavailable leaders. None of us are immune to missing a good night's sleep. Paying attention to how you react following a restless night is important. You deserve to have a restful night sleep. It's easy to accept "this is the way it is." My wish for you is that you delve into this more. Consider joining a breathing, meditation, or yoga class. Hire a naturopath doctor to support you. Perhaps your thyroid or iron is off. Take this seriously. You are worth it!

In your Emotionally Fit Room (Chapter 5, see Figure 2), I shared how H.A.L.T.E. (Hungry, Angry, Lonely, Tired or haven't had Exercise) had been a game changer for my clients. When they feel anxious, overwhelmed, out of sorts or second guess themselves, they check whether they have taken care of their H.A.L.T.E. If they are too tired for example, they try to defer a decision until they are more fully rested so they can make a better decision.

When I hear leaders are sending staff e-mails at midnight, 3 a.m. or even 5 a.m., I find it intimidating. Create the e-mail if you must, but save it and give yourself a reminder to send it out the next morning. Building a healthy work culture means investing in yourself to be that power of example. Your actions speak louder than your words.

You can explain how you have sleep troubles or you work best at night, however the undercurrent message is you *are* your work. You are defined by your role. A high standard of work ethic is demonstrated here. And it is unrealistic. I have heard it so many times from staff about how they feel guilty because they are leaving at the scheduled time rather than staying late or coming in early like their boss. If your employee is caring for an aging parent or child, or has their own health issues, your early morning or late-night e-mails only add pressure to them. Being flexible with rescheduling (when possible) any decision-making or critical thinking will help. When your tank is almost empty, it is hard to take a long trip. Taking time to refuel will help.

Owning your power by being tuned into your sleep patterns and taking necessary action to regulate and support your quality of sleep will pay dividends. Equally important is tuning into your staff's sleep patterns. Including them in the decision-making process regarding the best time to plan, meet, or update includes empowering them to say, "I haven't had enough sleep. Can we reschedule this please?" Have open conversations about best sleep practices. Make the importance of quality sleep a part of your healthy culture; it's no different than bringing in healthy food choices.

When you don't get enough sleep, you are left feeling fatigued which then leads to poor judgment, lack of self-control, and hinders your creativity. And if gaining weight isn't bad enough, you crave salty foods, and are more likely to give in to cravings. Sadly, if some simple changes aren't implemented, you will continue to wake up tired and carry that feeling of fatigue into your day and the day after and so on the cycle continues. When your energy plummets in the afternoon, you will attempt to wake up by indulging in more coffee or perhaps a sugar fix.

Good Sleep Hygiene

Think back to when you were a kid. When it came to sleep, did you have a bedtime routine? Did you wash your face and hands, brush your teeth, slip into your pajamas and jump into bed with anticipation of reading your favourite book? Maybe you said your prayers. And let's not forget the snuggles or hugs you received from your parent or caregiver. *Ah, the power of positive thoughts before you drift off to sleep.*

A study from the University of Manchester found that people who drifted off to sleep with positive thoughts slept longer and reported better sleep quality than people with negative thoughts. The cool part is that you can train yourself to flip the switch from negative to positive thoughts by simply using positive talk before bed.[37]

Let's fast track to common bedtime routines today. Many people stay up later either doing work or escaping into Netflix and fall into bed often past their ideal bedtime. The bedroom that was once a sacred space and time for relaxation, recharging, and resetting has now been replaced with TVs, laptops, and cell phones. Stimulation surrounds you as you attempt to fall asleep and stay asleep. Your mind needs downtime. It needs to take a vacation from your busy day. In light of the previous statistics of leaders having less sleep than the average person, I highly recommend you try the sleep routine outlined in Exercise 18. Now before you start resisting me, let me ask one question. "What would it mean to you to wake up refreshed, calm, confident, full of energy, creativity, and joy, ready to embrace your day?

Exercise 18
BUILD A BEDTIME ROUTINE

It has been said it takes 21 days to form a habit. There is competing research on this, but let's give 21 days a try. Commit to these routines for the next 21 days and see if you feel any different.

- Declutter your bedroom so it is welcoming, relaxing, and comforting.
- Remove all technology – TV, laptop, cell phone.
- Ensure your room is completely dark – no radio lights or cell phone screens – black out curtains help.
- Avoid caffeine after 3 p.m.
- Minimize your food intake after 7 p.m., especially processed sugar.
- Walk or engage in physical activity at least 3-4 hours before bed.
- Consistently go to bed at the same ideal time every night.
- Read or listen to a soothing meditation.
- Wake up at the same time each morning (7-9 hours of sleep is ideal).
- Greet your day with meditation or prayer.
- Review your gratitude list.
- Journal what you need to do, any swirling thoughts.

A great exercise I learned many years ago to help me sleep well is very easy to do. Lie on your back on your bed and tighten all the muscles in your body, one by one.

1. Start by scrunching up your toes, then tensing your legs.
2. Pull your belly button towards your back, letting your buttocks come slightly off the bed.
3. Next make fists with your hands, and tighten your arms as they lie close to your body.

4. Bring your shoulders to your ears.
5. Finally scrunch up your face like I am making you eat worms.
6. Take a deep breath from the bottom of your belly, hold it, and then release it slowly.
7. And relax your body.

Do this exercise as many times as you need in order to release the tension from your body. It will help you to relax and prepare you for a night of slumber.

Speaking from experience, if I haven't slept well the previous night, my judgement is impaired. I am likely more sensitive and risk being reactive if I am not careful. I am protective of my sleep for this reason. Being the best version of myself is important and coming from a place of kindness, confidence and clarity matters to me, as I am sure it does to you.

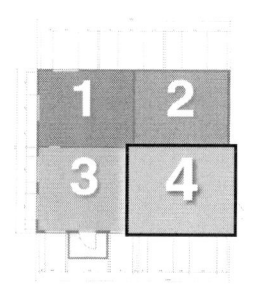

Room Four

YOUR SPIRITUALLY FIT ROOM

It's time to enter your fourth and final Room – your Spiritually Fit Room.

This Room is the foundation of all Four Rooms. When you think about building a house, the foundation is critical for the house to stand solid and secure. You do the same thing for your own powerhouse leadership. As you check into each Room, you become more connected, calmer, and centred, and you build a strong foundation – your Spiritually Fit Room.

Check into your Mentally Fit Room to quiet your mind, and to become aware and retrain your thoughts to help you rather than harm you. Then check into your Emotionally Fit Room to make that daily head-heart connection to tune into how you feel and what you need. Next, check into your Physically Fit Room to listen to your body's cues of when it needs rest, to move, or to be nourished with food. And finally, check into your Spiritually Fit Room to tap into your inner resource and wisdom.

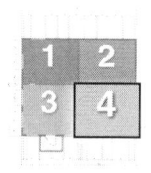

Chapter 16

What Does Being Spiritual Mean?

I attended a therapeutic horse workshop to support a friend who was getting certified. I was awestruck with the transformation that occurred between the participants and these massive beautiful beasts. I learned that horses in their natural state are prey, causing them to be fully present and aware of their surroundings. With our fast-paced world and all its distractions, we mere mortals are furthest from being in the precious present. I experienced first-hand how looking deep into a horse's eyes lets you touch your soul.

Inner Wisdom and Spirituality

Many of these horses engaged in these workshops suffered trauma or abuse and were heading to the glue factory to be killed. The exercises included participants being matched one-to-one with a horse to teach us the power of physical boundaries and how we often miss physical cues from subtle body language, how we stay in our head too long and miss the heart connection that allows us to tap into our inner wisdom along with other powerful lessons.

I met Jennifer while participating in this workshop. She had her arms crossed, her gaze down, and interacted minimally from the moment we started. I sensed something traumatic had happened to her. I kept my distance to respect her space, but offered support when needed. By the

---

Tap into the great wisdom within you. For more powerful exercises and solutions for your Spiritually Fit Room, visit my website: https://powerfuljourney.com/spirituallyfitroom

end of our day with the horses, Jennifer was like a different person. She practically skipped out of the barn and was smiling from ear to ear. What happened that shifted her you might be thinking?

The horses she worked with were able to mirror for Jennifer where she was stuck in her life and where she kept repeating old, unhealthy behaviours. In one instance, while in the arena with her horse, the horse repeatedly ran up to her and then ran away as if to tease her. Jennifer became aware that this is how she behaves in relationships. She shared how she is afraid to trust people or herself due to a long string of broken relationships. It was fascinating to watch. Once she shared this knowledge the horse came over to her and stayed by her side. She felt the message was that she needed to stay in the uncomfortable feelings and work through them rather than leaving mentally or physically when she is in a relationship.

It is hard to accurately describe the transformation that occurs when you work with a horse like this. I have since hired two therapeutic horse ranches in Costa Rica and Arizona to support the participants who hired me to facilitate their retreats. It was a highlight for each of them. One of the participants was asked to connect with a horse by standing outside his stall to observe and connect with him. He went to the opposite end of his stall and made such a ruckus, banging against the stall and gesturing to get out of it.

She was blown away by this experience. She had just said the day before in the group how she wanted to get out of her life (not literally) due to the stress and exhaustion from everyone wanting a piece of her. Her role as a social worker in her organization had depleted her energy and she had not been practicing self-care.

I highly recommend checking out these horse connection experiences.[38]

What Does Spirituality Mean to You?

Each of us has likely had an enlightening experience, but if we stay in our heads too much we may miss what is right in front of us. That experience may be sitting on a dock connecting with the serene surroundings of Mother Nature as calm and peace washes over you, it may have been the birth of a child, the death of a loved one, or the recovering of a relative from a serious illness or accident.

As French philosopher Pierre Teilhard de Chardin once said, "We are not human beings having a spiritual experience. We are spiritual beings having a human experience." And that experience means something different to each one of us. There is no right concept as spirituality is very personal and reflective of who we are at that given moment. Generally speaking, it includes a sense of connection to something bigger than us, and it typically involves a search for meaning in life. It is a universal human experience – something that touches us all.

> *Each of us has likely had an enlightening experience, but if we stay in our heads too much we may miss what is right in front of us.*

Viktor Frankl chronicled his experiences as a prisoner in Nazi concentration camps during World War II.[39] His psychotherapeutic method involved identifying a purpose in life to feel positive about, and then immersing yourself by imagining that outcome. According to Frankl, the way a prisoner imagined the future affected his longevity.

He reasoned that the inner hold a prisoner has on his spiritual self relies on having a hope in the future, and that once a prisoner loses that hope, he is doomed. He goes on to say, "What he (man) needs is not the discharge of tension at any cost but the call of a potential meaning waiting to be fulfilled by him."

So, what is spirituality for you? Is it being of service to others, connecting with nature, meditating or quieting your mind, attending church, being part of your church community, supporting a cause financially, or volunteering your talents? Defining what spirituality means to you will clarify what matters most when it comes to your spirit as well as feeling comfort in knowing that you are not alone in this life, that your life matters, and the power of experiencing peace and meaningful connection matters.

In my humble experience, the absence of a Higher Power in our professional roles is missing. I have been fortunate to work throughout North America and my experience has been that other countries outside Canada have a more integrated approach.

When speaking at a convention, one of the young participants died of a heart attack in her hotel room. The open dialogue about Higher Power was present. It seemed to offer participants comfort and solace during this difficult time of the death of their respected colleague. There was no pressure to believe in Higher Power, however there was a united connection in knowing there was something that supported them.

It seems the topic of spirituality has gotten so tense and sensitive that I wonder if we have swung the opposite way on the pendulum. Fear of excluding someone's faith or belief has left us paralyzed to include anything when a tragedy occurs at work, leaving a hole.

You, along with your team, will experience joy, relationship struggles, health challenges, mental health issues, addiction, conflict, or death. As their powerhouse leader, your team looks to you to lead them during uncertain times.

I heard of an organization where a staff member had committed suicide over the weekend. As you can imagine shock and grief ran rampant throughout the team. Their senior leader simply locked his office door and that was that. No discussion, no debrief. The message was loud and clear – move on. In another organization, a manager had a heart attack and died at work. A senior leader called me since I have authored two grief CDs and had worked with their team. We co-created a very special ritual. Staff were able to come into a welcoming room where we had flowers, a candle, coffee, and a massive card for them to share with the deceased's family how much their colleague or friend meant to them. This open exchange of how team members felt about their colleague brought meaning to their relationship. It also humanized the whole work experience when an organization chooses to make their people a priority in this way.

Too often I have worked with teams where their leader simply avoided the topic and carried on as if it was business as usual. My hope is you will rethink this choice if this is you. It's normal to feel uncomfortable or fearful about how to address a death, mental illness, divorce, or a controversial topic. Be transparent and share how you feel with your team. You don't have to have the answers. At the core of each one of us is the need to feel safe and supported. Most of us simply want a safe space to share how we feel. When a family crisis occurs, bringing everyone to the table to have an open discussion helps each member feel heard, supported, and connected rather than creating a story in their heads about what happened or why no one is sharing how they feel. Silence does more harm. How do you handle the Spiritually Fit Room?

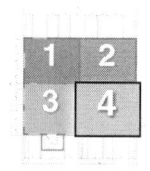

Chapter 17

Your Need for Meaningful Connection

Following a leadership team retreat I facilitated for a large mental health hospital, the CEO and I were talking about how it can get lonely at the top. When asked, "Who do you talk with to let your hair down and share your deepest fears or concerns – your business coach, your wife, or a friend?" He said, "No one. I keep it to myself."

Currently, we are experiencing a loneliness epidemic that needs our attention.

Loneliness Versus Alone

In Canada, studies have found that one in five Canadians identify as being lonely. According to Statistics Canada more and more people live alone, with 28% of households having one occupant.[40] According to a 2018 survey from *The Economist* and the Kaiser Family Foundation (KFF), more than two in ten adults in the United States (22%) and the United Kingdom (23%) say they always or often feel lonely, lack companionship, or feel left out or isolated, frequently with physical, mental, and financial consequences.[41] The scourge of loneliness is an issue that we're going to hear more about in the years to come.

Tap into the great wisdom within you. For more powerful exercises and solutions for your Spiritually Fit Room, visit my website: https://powerfuljourney.com/spirituallyfitroom

Please note there is a difference between being alone and loneliness. A person is alone when they are by themself. Loneliness is when a person is lonely, when she or he feels abandoned or sad due to isolation.

Ami Rokach, a psychologist at Toronto's York University who has studied loneliness for more than 30 years says, "The associated stigma often prevents those experiencing intense loneliness from seeking help."[42] "There is a stigma attached to being lonely. People would rather admit to being schizophrenic than admit to suffering from loneliness. ... The lonely person tells himself, 'I don't have anyone because I'm a loser.'"[43]

I don't know about you, but I have experienced situations where I am in a crowded room and, notwithstanding, felt lonely. Henry David Thoreau famously stated in *Walden* that "the mass of men lead lives of quiet desperation." Who do you know that appears to be in a great partnership or marriage and is experiencing loneliness? I would say we all know someone. An outside observer looking in would think they have it all together and have everything a person would want, however you know their spouse is unavailable physically, emotionally, or mentally due to work, travel, an addiction, or any number of things. Each of us has experienced bouts of loneliness, however, we are wired for meaningful human connection.

Here are some ideas from the Canadian Mental Health Association to help you find some connections.[44]

- Join a new club, or try out a group activity.
- Reach out to an old friend you've lost touch with.
- Volunteer for a cause you care about.
- Eat lunch in a communal space.
- Introduce yourself to your neighbours.
- Ask someone for help when you need it.
- Do a random act of kindness.

If this doesn't apply to you, is there someone in your life who could benefit from your time and attention to help them feel more connected and valued?

Connection Is Good for Your Health

A lack of meaningful human connection can be more harmful than obesity, smoking, inactivity, and high blood pressure. According to the Canadian Mental Health Association,

Social connection can lower anxiety and depression, help us regulate our emotions, lead to higher self-esteem and empathy, and actually improve our immune systems. By neglecting our need to connect, we put our health at risk.[45]

Our fast-paced world has us running from one activity to another and keeping up with its demands can be all consuming. Trying to strive for a balance of working long hours, driving your kids or parents to appointments or activities, volunteer work, interests, building in self-care, and so much more can leave you tired and overwhelmed. Sadly, the first item to be stroked off many people's calendars is social connections.

Think about a time when you cancelled your lunch or coffee date with a friend because you had too much on the go or you were overscheduled. Wouldn't that have been the very thing your spirit needed to fill up? Instead we lose ourselves in mindlessly scrolling through social media to "connect" with our friends, family, and colleagues. We get the illusion we are connecting when, in fact, we are mostly getting the "upbeat and happy news" versus the truth of what they are struggling with.

How often do you see couples or families at a restaurant or outing all glued to their technology? What was once totally unacceptable has become the norm.

What did it feel like when you were having a conversation with someone you cared about and they started texting or scrolling through their social media? Disconnected, unimportant, neglected, invisible? Becoming more consciously aware of our technology habits and when and where it is appropriate is important.

Being present requires more effort, yet the rewards are great. You experience a more meaningful connection with yourself *and* the other person. Creating a no technology zone or timeframe will help. When you build this into your routine it will allow you to connect in a more meaningful way.

Perhaps you are one of the lucky ones and are a highly connected person and others know the authentic you. Congratulations, this is wonderful. Some of the clients I have worked with have shared with me that their long hours and highly intense roles have impacted how and when they connect with the people they care about. Simple things like falling asleep during movie time, running late, or not being fully present at special celebrations due to fatigue or preoccupation of a work issue were a few of their challenges.

Imagine the impact it would have on your team if you invested in their Spiritually Fit Room by establishing one room at your office where they could check in to relax, reset, feel safe, and connect with themselves and their Higher Power. As a team they can brainstorm the look and feel of whatever room works best and what their primary goals are – from the colours on the wall to whether you could wear earphones to listen to a meditation or soft music to meditation colouring books with colour pencils to inspirational quotes on a board to any number of relaxing things to help achieve a more mindful state. Or if this doesn't fit, at least have the conversation on how best to cope with the stress of your ever-changing work culture.

This safe space to rest and recharge is a powerful message of hope that demonstrates you acknowledge the toll their work, their challenges, and their commitment to the people and the families that you serve has on their spirit. It can be tough work at times and having a leader who gets this matters.

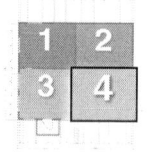

Chapter 18

Has Your Spiritual Growth Become Stunted?

The leaders I work with are often seasoned, very bright, accomplished, and respected – much like you. Commonly, what has blocked them is forgetting the power of who they are. They spent so many years with their head down, lost in their work, and providing the best quality service and support for their teams and their communities that their Spiritually Fit Room is often neglected and they've suffered.

Some don't check in for many weeks, months, or even years. I remember one saying she felt like a donut with a hole in her soul. Others felt they were spiritually bankrupt. Others felt they dabbled once in a while. Whether you check into your Spiritually Fit Room regularly or sporadically, my invitation to you is to make it a priority. You owe it to yourself to invest in yourself in this way.

Blocking Your Spirit

Avoiding unresolved grief will surely block your spirit. With every loss comes grief, a natural process that is our human way of emotional healing. But all too often this normal process gets compartmentalized or pushed underground. Our society rewards workaholism and being busy. Workaholism is a perfect way to hide, to avoid feeling the pain of an estranged

---

Tap into the great wisdom within you. For more powerful exercises and solutions for your Spiritually Fit Room, visit my website: https://powerfuljourney.com/spirituallyfitroom

friendship, a relationship ending, the death of a loved one, or massive changes to your organization or your life.

With every loss comes grief, a natural process that is our human way of emotional healing.

When I was doing the research for my two grief CDs that address the loss of an estranged relationship or the death of a loved one, patterns of avoidance showed up for many busy leaders. You can only keep a lid on the unresolved grief for so long. Eventually the top blows off.

Signs you have unresolved grief can show up in a sudden outburst, obsessive thinking of your loved one, or excessive use of food, alcohol, drugs, sleep aids, or other high-risk behaviour to try to numb your pain. You may become weepy during unexpected times, like commercials, or you become needy or obsessed with where your family or friends are for fear of them dying too. For others it's a feeling of numbness; they feel disconnected from the loss. For some, they get caught up in overreactions of anger or judgement that is out of character for them.

Typically, this person is in protection mode, wanting to prevent further loss or pain. "I will push you away first, before you hurt or leave me like so-and-so did when they died or left me." Pay attention to the patterns in your relationships. Are you someone who embraces your grief head on, or do you give yourself a deadline for when you need to "be over it," or do you forge ahead and suck it up because you don't have time to feel?

Feel it now or feel it later. Grief doesn't go away. It manifests in self-destructive ways that block you from fully embracing the joy, connection, and love in your life. When you give yourself permission to grieve, be sure to surround yourself with supportive people. Work with a grief counsellor or therapist, attend a retreat that focuses on healing from the death of a loved one or a relationship that ended, read books specific to the grief you are experiencing, or participate in a grief group related to your situation. There is power in numbers whether you choose an online support group or an in-person one.

Another common way to block your spirit from the light is to be totally self-reliant. This self-protective behaviour disconnects you not only from your Higher Power, but from the people that matter most. At the core of complete self-reliance is a mistrust that you can't count on anyone but yourself. After all, it's easier to do things yourself, then you know they will get done right. Perfectionism plays a role here (see Chapter 8, Setting

Healthy Boundaries). How will others ever measure up to your expectations if they are never given the opportunity to try it their way.

You are here for a reason. You bring your unique gifts and talents. Perhaps you already know why you are here. Or maybe you have lost your way. Or maybe you have not yet discovered your purpose.

Be patient. Be aware. Be curious.

A Gratitude Attitude Mindset

Another important approach or strategy is having a gratitude attitude in action within your work culture. Is volunteering encouraged and supported within your team? Are you volunteering for a special project or fundraiser that is aligned with your values? The passion found from engaging in acts of kindness and gratitude is profound.

Gratitude is our emotion that relates to our ability to feel and express thankfulness and appreciation. Traditionally, the study of this emotion has been typically found in the fields of theology and philosophy. In 2007, Robert Emmons began researching gratitude through a psychological lens. He found that expressing gratitude improves mental, physical, and relational well-being. Being grateful also impacts the overall experience of happiness, and these effects tend to be long-lasting.[46]

Each of us has had experiences where we were overwhelmed with gratitude. Our child or loved one recovers from an illness or accident, we get support from a friend at just the right time, we ace a paper or a project, the test results came out great, we hear of a dying friend and are grateful for our own health, or any number of things. The power of gratitude connects us to ourselves, each other, nature, and our Higher Power.

> *The power of gratitude connects us to ourselves, each other, nature, and our Higher Power.*

When you drop into your heart to appreciate the many things you are grateful for it results in a positive and hopeful present and future. There are any number of ways to show gratitude. (Try the gratitude challenge in Exercise 19.) I know of one leader who writes personal notes each month to her staff, specifically sharing her gratitude on how they handled something well or how they showed up when they were needed most.

I have used a gratitude exercise within a team retreat that entails team members passing around a cue card or full sheet of paper with one of their colleague's names on it. Each team member writes specifically how they were most grateful for them. An example would be, "I appreciate how you ask me about my weekend, Frank. I feel connected to you."

Another way is to keep a gratitude journal and write in it each day what specifically you are most grateful for. I recently read of a man who decided to keep an annual gratitude journal for his wife and gave it to her at Thanksgiving. Each day he noted something he was grateful for or something she said or did that warmed his heart. As you can imagine she said this was the best gift he could have ever given her. Although her very positive reaction was a bonus, he felt he had benefited the most. By seeing his wife in this light, it allowed him to not sweat the small stuff in their relationship. We all know that it can be the small stuff where we explode, not necessarily the big stuff.

I worked in a health unit for years where we had Secret Santa's or Secret Friends. All the names of those staff members who are participating get their name put into a hat. A draw is done and you are given a person's name, in this case, for a month. Each week you secretly deliver a small gift or token of appreciation for that person to connect on a deeper level. You pay close attention to what hot or cold drinks they have, to what treats they enjoy, to what activities bring them joy. At the end of the month, we had a potluck and had to guess who our secret friend was. It was so simple and fun and brought us all together. It lightened our heavy workloads.

When I was struggling with a relationship with a friend where I felt it was one sided and the person was negative, one of my mentor's suggested I keep a jar in my kitchen. Each time this friend said or did something kind or loving towards me, I was to write it down on a piece of paper and put it in the jar. The more I focused on how I was grateful for this person, the more the tension from my end subsided. I started to not take the comments so personally and began looking through a different lens. The perceived criticism was more about that person's own fears and doubts that were projected onto me. I began to see this friend in a very different light.

Some leaders I have worked with begin or end their team or staff meetings with each member sharing something they are grateful for. When each of us gets into that heart space of being grateful and being more mindful there is a shift in the energy and focus within the group.

Pay attention to the feedback in your team and your life. When it's crunch time for a deadline, keeping a gratitude exchange going with all the ways you are empowering your body, mind, and spirit to be at your optimum health helps.

Exercise 19

THE 21-DAY GRATITUDE CHALLENGE

Engage your team with a 21-day gratitude challenge. This keeps the focus on what's working well versus what isn't working well. It will reduce or eliminate gossip, engage people to bring out the best in each other with a simple thank you and acts of appreciation, and it will connect your team in an even more meaningful way.

When you as their powerhouse leader take time out of your busy day to thank your employees, in turn your employees feel more motivated to work harder. They will experience more joy, connection, and be more engaged.

Your Gratitude List

_____

_____

_____

_____

_____

What gratitude activities do you participate in?

Drop into your heart? How does it feel having written what you are grateful for?

When you are focused on the good in your life, coupled with acknowledging that the source of this goodness is partly outside yourself, you are able to set your spirit free. Yes, it's good to learn about spirituality through reading books, but experiencing it as a spirit connection is something much deeper.

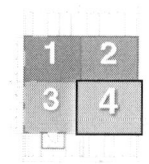

Chapter 19

The Positive Impact of Mindfulness

Merriam-Webster defines mindfulness as "the practice of maintaining a nonjudgmental state of heightened or complete awareness of one's thoughts, emotions, or experiences on a moment-to-moment basis." Basically, mindfulness means being aware of and controlling your experience. You are consciously aware and respond to your world from that place.

Think of a time when you drove to work or drove home from work, and you have no recall of the trip in between. Or a colleague or team member was sharing something with you and your mind was somewhere else and you missed the whole message. When your brain is in overdrive and you are caught up in the "to-do list" being present may be difficult.

The Benefits

According to the Centre for Mindfulness Studies, the benefits of mindfulness include:

- stress reduction,
- reduced rumination,
- decreased negative affect (e.g. depression, anxiety),
- less emotional reactivity or more effective emotion regulation,

---

Tap into the great wisdom within you. For more powerful exercises and solutions for your Spiritually Fit Room, visit my website: https://powerfuljourney.com/spirituallyfitroom

- increased focus,
- more cognitive flexibility, and
- improved working memory.[47]

The regular practice of mindfulness routines can reduce mental wandering and distractibility. Your routine may include regular deep breathing breaks where you sit and focus on your breath, or scheduled meditation times. Checking into your Spiritually Fit Room allows you to be sure you are aligned with the purpose of why you are here.

When I worked with Janice, she was a manager of a not-for-profit organization. She was a breath of fresh air according to her team when she was hired. She spent much of her first several months listening, listening to what her staff was saying and not saying. Once trust was developed, she began asking questions of her staff about what they were passionate about. What made their heart sing?

She began matching those passions within their work roles. If someone loved working with seniors, she created space for that person to spend time with seniors within their organization in a meaningful way and within their mandate. Other staff had other talents and dreams and she was intentional of how she supported them and included this in their work. Her willingness to pay witness to what they wanted and what interests they had paid off immensely. Her once tired and overworked team were revived by her commitment to tap into their individual desires and dreams. When you check into your Spiritually Fit Room and take action, connection, joy, a renewed sense of purpose, and energy arises. What a perfect example!

When your life is lopsided and the majority of your thoughts, feelings, and actions are centered around your work, other areas of your life suffer as do your Four Rooms.

Some leaders I work with are active in their churches or spiritual communities. Others are passionate about connecting with Mother Nature and support the well-being of Mother Nature by signing petitions for government change, organizing or participating in community clean ups, and participating in lobby groups to effect change in their city or their country. Others volunteer in their community. If a relative has experienced support from a particular organization or hospital they may volunteer on a fundraising committee to give back or honour their loved one.[48]

Tapping into Your Mindfulness

Meditation practice is a beautiful way to check into your Spiritually Fit Room (see Exercise 20). When you press that pause button and embrace the silence, it allows your higher self to emerge.

In the book, *The Power of Flow*, the authors share that when you learn to quiet your mind, you are able to listen to your intuition.[49]

I love that the word "silent" is an anagram for "listen."

Exercise 20
WHAT DOES YOUR SPIRITUALLY FIT ROOM NEED?

Take some time to reflect on your Spiritually Fit Room. What does it need right now?

Write down the needs and wishes for your Spiritually Fit Room. Here are some suggestions to mull over to help you decide.

- Whether you are connected to a spiritual teacher or are on the search for one, I encourage you to think about what is missing in your life?
- Would connecting with a meditation teacher help quiet your busy mind and provide a much-needed practice of stillness?
- Have you gotten away from attending that yoga class you used to participate in?
- Are you actively involved in an interest or hobby that allows you to express yourself through art?
- What is on your "I'll get to it one of these days" list? Taking a photography course, bird watching, gardening, hiking, joining a cycling group, or getting lost in a fabulous book that takes you places?
- Has travel been on that list, but it keeps getting shelved?

_____

_____

_____

Indian philosopher Sri Aurobindo said intuition is "a memory of Truth." It's that knowingness you have about something or someone without having all the facts.

I love that the word "silent" is an anagram for "listen."

Some refer to it as a "gut feeling." You likely have someone in your life that is good at acting on these hunches or intuitive wisdom. The practice of mindfulness allows you to tune in and build on your intuitive skills on a much deeper level to support you being that powerhouse leader.

Creating space in your day to "just be" will support your overall health and well-being to feed your soul. It will allow you to reflect, recharge, and reset yourself.

If any of this feels overwhelming or intimidating, I am a huge fan of a day or weekend retreat. This will allow you to ease into becoming more mindful. As I shared earlier, I have been both facilitating and attending retreats for over 15 years. Prepare yourself, for once you attend a really good retreat there is no turning back. This is mind candy in its healthiest form. You will want more. This is a commitment I make twice a year to myself to allow me to make myself a priority, create the framework for me to let go, and explore my Spiritual Room on a whole new level.[50]

When in your life have you naively felt you have all the time in the world to take that course, try a new hobby, volunteer for a charity that matters to you, or take that yoga class only to realize there is no better time than this moment? How often have you wondered where the time went? It's winter, and now it's summer and you question what happened to spring? I love the Lee Ann Womack song, "I Hope You Dance."[51] It reminds you to just be in the moment and, yes, dance. Not when you complete the deadline or when the kids are in bed or you finished your calls, dance now. Dance like nobody's watching. Be *free*. Be *carefree*. You are worth it.

For some leaders, their Spiritually Fit Room was rundown due to all the responsibilities and pressure they put on themselves. When they came up for air during a sick day or sick leave, they were unaware of how they had become human doers rather than human beings. They spent so much time in their head that they missed out on the greatest journey they will ever experience, the journey from their head to their heart.

Think of someone who is truly connected with their head and their heart. How do they show up differently for you? Would you say they are fully present? They are actively listening to you instead of thinking about the wise words they need to impart on you. They are real. They are authentic, right?

"Wherever you are, be there," is a mantra I created some years ago to remind me that being in the precious present is the greatest gift I can give myself and those around me. When I do that, I am able to see the people in my life. I love the line in the science fiction movie, *Avatar*,[52] where the Na'vi people greet each other with, "I see you." The clan's philosophy is to open the mind and heart to the present and embrace Pandora as if seeing it for the very first time.

It's common for many people to check into their Spiritually Fit Room when they experience a tragedy, trauma, or health issue with themselves or a loved one. They desperately cry out to the Higher Power of their understanding for help or comfort. I think that it's great that they are reaching out to something greater than themselves to support them through their difficult time. Has this been you at some point in your life?

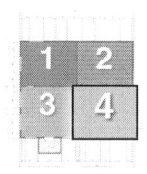

Chapter 20

Let Go, Let Joy In

When was the last time you fully and completely let go? As a leader keeping it all together requires you to be in action mode much of the time. Your body takes its orders from your thoughts. For some, letting go is frightening, maybe even terrifying. When you let go you are allowing your spirit to be vulnerable and to trust. Trust yourself. Trust the person you are with. And trust the process.

If trust is something that is hard for you because someone along the way broke your trust, then letting go will look different for you. However, it is achievable and, I will go as far as saying, your sense of well-being depends on you to figure this out. Trust and letting go are first cousins. Letting go has many layers to it, much like an onion.

Peeling Back the Layers

The only way to see those layers is to connect with them. What area in your life do you struggle with letting go? Is it your intimate relationships or work relationships? Is it relationships from your past or current? The human brain compartmentalizes all your memories to help keep you safe. When you are ready the memory or situation will appear for you to deal with whatever is needed to let go. Letting go requires effort. You are worth the effort.

Tap into the great wisdom within you. For more powerful exercises and solutions for your Spiritually Fit Room, visit my website: https://powerfuljourney.com/spirituallyfitroom

I know when I have taken my will back, when I try to control things, when I judge others or myself, I focus on the problem. I see no way out and begin to feel hopeless in a situation. Or I stay stuck in being a victim or a martyr. Letting go breathes life into my spirit.

When you let go of what's not serving you, you make room for the good things to come in. In Melody Beattie's awesome book, *The Language of Letting Go*, she mentions that a client asked her, "How do I handle the good stuff? It's harder and more foreign than the pain and tragedy." Melody's reply was, "The same way you handled the difficult and the painful experiences, one day at a time."[53]

> *When you let go of what's not serving you, you make room for the good things to come in.*

Keep in mind all that you have is today. It's when you get preoccupied in regrets from yesterday and fear of what tomorrow will bring that you break down. As a mentor, when students get engrossed in their story of what they are fretting about for something they fear will happen next week, next year, or sometime in their lifetime, I ask them, "What day are you in?" This question is my attempt to interrupt their Hollywood story of what could happen in order to shift their thinking to what they have control over – today. Typically, giggles follow.

Where in your thinking have you been wearing out your spirit and giving away your power to something or someone that you have little control over? Are you thinking about today or is it yesterday or tomorrow?

Finding the Joy

Writing a joy list is a great way to help you become aware of what you enjoy (see Exercise 21). Leaders have shared with me that during periods when they have spent a lot of time at the office, they feel depleted and unclear of what brings them joy. Letting your joy list be an evolving document will help you when checking into your Spiritually Fit Room. What makes your heart sing?

As you review the things on your joy list what feelings come up? Happiness, joy, gratitude, excitement? By giving yourself permission to write this list you are choosing to fill your spirit up. Congratulations! Now you have an evolving list of what brings you joy. Next is to do it.

Exercise 21

THE JOY LIST

Take a moment now. Set a timer for 15 minutes and write all the things that fill your spirit up and bring you joy. (Personally, I like writing this with a pen and paper rather than typing, however you find what works best for you.)

You can ask people closest to you "what brings you joy or what fills your spirit up" to gather ideas for your list.

Keep this joy list close. When your spirit feels tired or overwhelmed, pull out your list and do one of them. This reset will deposit joy into your spirit and energize you.

My Joy List

_____   _____
_____   _____
_____   _____
_____   _____
_____   _____
_____   _____

Give yourself permission to do something each day from your list. If belly laughing is something you love to do, then schedule it in your calendar. Connect with a friend who you love to laugh with or watch that funny TV show that helps you to let go and belly laugh.

Reading a captivating book and drinking that hot cup of tea or coffee, dancing or singing like nobody's watching, or being engrossed in some form of art can be uplifting activities for many people. Gardening is a powerful spirit connection for me, as I am immersed with Mother Nature. Secretly, pulling weeds out is such a release; it's like getting rid of the weeds in my life – people, activities, and things that I need to let go of or detach from. Many people talk about the power of a great nature walk and how their perspective shifts upon their return.

We have all experienced spiritual teachers. It may be your pastor, a guru, healer, meditation teacher, yoga instructor, an artist, your family pet, or any number of spiritual leaders or teachers. What words of wisdom or sage advice have they provided that you carry around with you (see Exercise 22)?

Exercise 22
SAGE WORDS

Take out a note pad.

What inspiring sage words have you heard from your spiritual teachers that have lifted your spirit and helped you let go?

Here are some of the sage words that I have heard.
- I am a safe.
- Life happens *for* me, not *to* me.
- All is well. Everything serves.

Sage Words

_____

_____

_____

_____

_____

_____

_____

_____

I have found huge benefits in both being a mentor and having a mentor. Find someone who shares similar values and walks their talk to the best of their ability.

"The teacher appears when the student is ready." Is there someone who comes to mind who would be a great fit to be your mentor? Reach out and schedule a coffee date and open the conversation up.

You may be unclear as to what your spirit needs right now because you are so tired. I was once that Type A leader who poured everything into my work and often returned home completely drained. My poor family got my energy leftovers. My spirit was depleted. Until I burned out some years later, I was in warrior mode for the people we served, however there was a price to pay. There are times when you are pulled in so many directions, how can you become your own priority (see Exercise 23).

Exercise 23
PERMISSION TO BE YOUR OWN PRIORITY

Write down the answer to this question as you check into your Spiritually Fit Room.

"What will fill my spirit up in this moment?"

Now do it!

Here is your permission slip to allow you to make yourself a priority, allow you to discover other parts of yourself, and to allow you to fill up your spirit.

This permission slip gives _____ permission to participate in self-care (hot shower/soak), read an escape book, dancing, walking in nature. They deserve it. ♥

Final Thoughts

Knowing you have a right to sit at the leadership table is a big part of being that powerhouse leader. Keeping the imposter at bay will be dependent on checking into and taking daily action in your Four Rooms – your Mentally, Emotionally, Physically, and Spiritually Fit Rooms. Vitality, joy, focus, confidence, and peace of mind will be your reward.

Be extra vigilant and plan ahead when you have a looming deadline where you are stretched and putting in multitudes of hours. By applying these powerhouse health habits they will help you pace your time and energy, and allow you to focus. It will prevent burn out. These simple health habits compound over time.

Take full responsibility for all the choices you make. The significant people in your life are fully responsible for their lives too. Give them the dignity to make their own mistakes and experience the confidence of navigating their lives. This is an act of detaching with love, not selfishness, on your part. This frees you up to get to know you.

Happiness is an inside job. Be your own best champion. Give yourself permission to play and be silly. This prevents you from letting your knickers get in a knot and staying in your head too long.

Thriving as a powerhouse leader requires discipline. The temptation to fall off the wagon and turn to processed sugar, excessive amounts of caffeine, junk food, and carbohydrates will be there coupled with obsessing over mistakes, beating yourself up, and judging yourself. Be gentle with yourself. Treat yourself like you are somebody you care about. Pushed yourself too hard or had unrealistic expectations of yourself? Not to worry. You can do a reset anytime of the day.

Planning ahead personally and as an organization will prevent this from happening. Start with the end in mind. How do you/we want to feel when accreditation is finished, when the proposal is sent, the hiring or firing process is complete, or whatever deadline exists? Pay attention to the feedback from your body, mind, and spirit. Bring in fruits, vegetables, and other healthy foods. Drink loads of lemon water to energize you rather than pop or caffeine that deplete you when your optimum brain power and energy is needed the most. Let your thinking and actions be part of the solution not the problem.

Simple success habits like creating a morning ritual, such as the Power of Four Morning Routine, will help.

1. Ground yourself by meditation or deep breathing.
2. Move your body with yoga or strength training or brisk walk.
3. Drop into your heart and feel the gratitude you have for a minimum of three things.
4. Set your intention for the day. Be clear how you want to show up for that day. Make sure being present is part of this.

End your day by reflecting on your accomplishments and make note of where you can be better the next day. This helps you sleep better.

Sleep deprivation is very real and affects your body, mind, and spirit. You lose focus, gain weight, make more mistakes, and it weakens your immune system, sucking the life out of you. Remember to remove all technology from your bedroom (unless on call of course) and let your bedtime routine be predictable, relaxing, peaceful, and something you look forward to. Read that engaging book, journal how you are feeling to release the day's events, or listen to a meditation CD. Let this nurturing sleep routine be soothing and self-compassionate.

Accept that self-doubts are part of the process. The more competent you are, the more self-doubts you will have. Your leadership role and becoming the best version of yourself is evolving.

Ask yourself daily, "What would I choose if I loved myself in this situation?" Mastering your mindset as a leader has a rippling effect on your team. Ongoing education, like training, leadership or life coaching, therapy, retreats, self-help and business books, will be your learning classroom. I want to say it one more time. Attend retreats that fill your soul up and help you let go of the things that rob you of your power. Commit to regular team retreats to celebrate, recharge, and reset your team's goals.

Be curious. Try different things. Much like a buffet table, take what you want and leave what you don't want. You might tuck it away for a later time when you are ready or when someone you care about needs it.

Be open. Be open and accepting of your mistakes. They are all part of the journey. Oftentimes it's your mistakes that grace you with the greatest lessons and wisdom.

Be willing. Be willing to do whatever it takes to be that powerhouse leader. That may be learning to be more vulnerable as you get to know yourself in a deeper way. It may be saying "No" more often so you can create space for "Yes" in your life. Ask for help when you need it and share your anxiety and fears with people you trust. We are meant to walk this journey together. You are not alone. It may mean having more courageous conversations with yourself and others about what serves you well and what doesn't.

Be humble. Connect with the quietness of your heart where you know all is well and everything serves a purpose. Within that peace, rest your weary spirit even when no one is praising you or singing your accolades. Be one with your Higher Power in knowing that you are enough, and you are safe.

Be kind. Be kind with yourself as you continue to stretch and grow. Celebrate your successes often. This, my friend, gives you wings to fly and be that powerhouse leader you are meant to be.

Endnotes

Awakening Your Power

[1] Victor Fleming (director), *The Wizard of Oz* (Metro-Goldwyn-Mayer Studios Inc., 1939).

Chapter 1: **What's Power Got to Do with Being a Leader?**

[2] Robert Anthony, *Beyond Positive Thinking: A No-Nonsense Formula for Getting the Results You Want* (Garden City, NY: Morgan James, 2004).

[3] Patrick Lencioni, *The 5 Dysfunctions of a Team: A Leadership Fable* (Jossey-Bass, 2002).

[4] "God, grant me the serenity to accept the things I cannot change. The courage to change the things I can and the wisdom to know the difference."

[5] Melody Beattie, *The Language of Letting Go* (Hazleton Foundation, 1990).

Chapter 2: **What Does It Mean to Be a Powerhouse?**

[6] Moving forward, I will use the term "Higher Power," however, fill in the word that works best for you. It may be Creator, Spirit, Mother Nature, God, Universe or the acronym G.O.D. (Good Orderly Direction). It may be an it, female, male, or have no gender attached at all. In the movie, *The Shack*, God was represented as a caring, loving, and compassionate black woman. You decide.

[7] Nancy Meyers (director), *The Holiday* (Columbia Pictures, 2006).

Chapter 3: **Mental Blind Spots**

[8] Guy Finley, *The Secret of Letting Go* (Llewellyn Publications, 2007).

[9] In 1978, researchers Dr. Pauline R. Clance and Dr. Suzanne A. Imes first coined the phrase Imposter phenomenon (IP). See: Pauline R. Clance, and Suzanne A. Imes, "The Impostor Phenomenon in High Achieving Women: Dynamics and Therapeutic Intervention." *Psychotherapy: Theory, Research & Practice* (Fall 1978) 15 (3): 241–247. Studies on this syndrome continue. A June 2016 study showed that social influences and perfectionism are significant predictors for imposter syndrome as traditional graduate students showed a higher IP score than online students. See: Christy B. Fraenza, "The Role of Social Influence in Anxiety and the Imposter Phenomenon" Online Learning Journal (June 2016) 20(2): 230-243 (DOI: http://dx.doi.org/10.24059/olj.v20i2.618).

[10] Jack Canfield, Coauthor of the New York Times Bestselling *Chicken Soup for the Soul*® series and *The Success Principles: How to Get from Where You Are to Where You Want to Be*™

[11] Eyal Ophir, Clifford Nass, and Anthony D. Wagner, "Cognitive Control in Media Multitaskers." *Proceedings of the National Academy of Sciences of the United States of America* (September 15, 2009) 106 (37): 15583-15587 (https://doi.org/10.1073/pnas.0903620106)

[12]Kendra Cherry, "How Multitasking Affects Productivity and Brain Health" (March 26, 2020) on verywellmind.com.

Chapter 6: Freedom from Guilt
[13]Don Miguel Ruiz, *The Four Agreements: A Practical Guide to Personal Freedom* (Amber-Allen Publishing, 1997).

Chapter 7: Let Go of What Isn't Serving You and Forgive
[14]Lila Larson, *Small Business, Big Growth: 50 Ways to Get Clear, Get Focused and Get Better Results* (Winnipeg, MB, 2015).

[15]Brené Brown, *The Gifts of Imperfection: Let Go of Who You Think You're Supposed to Be and Embrace Who You Are* (Minnesota: Hazelden Publishing, 2010).

[16]"How Holding Grudges Can Shorten Your Life and How to Move On" (May 2, 2019) (https://www.neurocorecenters.com/blog/holding-grudges-can-shorten-life-move).

[17]Louise Hay, *You Can Heal Your Life* (Hay House Inc., 1984), p. 159.

Chapter 9: Surround Yourself with Powerhouse People
[18]Shakespeare, *Hamlet*, 1.3.78.

Chapter 10: Love Yourself Now, Not When
[19]Foundation for Inner Peace, *A Course in Miracles* (1975).

Chapter 11: What Is Your Body Trying to Tell You?
[20]Gabor Maté, *When the Body Says No: The Cost of Hidden Stress* (Toronto: Vintage Canada, 2003).

Chapter 12: How Are You Self-Protecting While Under Stress?
[21]See: Healthline.com.

[22]Liudmila Gamaiunova, et. al., "Exploration of Psychological Mechanisms of the Reduced Stress Response in Long-Term Meditation Practitioners" *Psychoneuroendocrinology*, volume 104 (June 2019), pp. 143-151.

[23]Laurie K. Twells, Ph.D., et. al., "Current and Predicted Prevalence of Obesity in Canada: A Trend Analysis" CMAL Open March 3, 2014, vol. 2, no. 1, pp. E18-E26 (DOI: 10.9778/cmajo.20130016).

[24]Press Release (December 18, 2019): "Close to half of U.S. population projected to have obesity by 2030" (https://www.hsph.harvard.edu/news/press-releases/half-of-us-to-have-obesity-by-2030/).

[25]See: https://www.heartandstroke.ca/-/media/pdf-files/canada/2017-position-statements/obesity-ps-eng.ashx?la=en&hash=E02733A55849E27F47F82314C389F55C5777.

[26]The Dennison's created Educational Kinesiology (Edu-K) – enhanced learning through movement. This led to the unique learning-readiness program known as Brain Gym®, a proprietary programme of body movements.

[27] Harvard Health Publishing, "The Heart Attack Gender Gap" (April 2016): https://www.health.harvard.edu/heart-health/the-heart-attack-gender-gap.

[28] The Heart and Stroke Foundation of Canada signs of a heart attack.

[29] Centre for Addiction and Mental Health, "Workplace Mental Health: A Review and Recommendations" (January 2020): https://www.camh.ca/-/media/files/workplace-mental-health/workplacementalhealth-a-review-and-recommendations-pdf.pdf?la=en&hash=5B04D442283C004D0FF4A05E3662F39022268149

Chapter 13: Nourishing Your Body with Healthy Foods

[30] Dr. Michael Rahman, naturopathic doctor, Pinewood Natural Health Centre: superfood list.

[31] James. L. Wilson, *Adrenal Fatigue: The 21st Century Stress Syndrome* (Smart Publications, 2001).

Chapter 14: Your Health Is in the Toilet

[32] Piedmont Healthcare, "What Your Stool Says About Your Health" (https://www.piedmont.org/living-better/what-your-stool-says-about-your-health).

[33] Canadian Society for Exercise Physiology, "Canadian Physical Activity Guidelines" found at: https://csep.ca/CMFiles/Guidelines/CSEP_PAGuidelines_0-65plus_en.pdf.

[34] Joe Leech, "7 Science-Based Health Benefits of Drinking Enough Water" (June 30, 2020) on Healthline.com (https://www.healthline.com/nutrition/7-health-benefits-of-water).

Chapter 15: Sleep Matters

[35] Centers for Disease Control and Prevention, "1 in 3 Adults Don't Get Enough Sleep" (February 16, 2016) (https://www.cdc.gov/media/releases/2016/p0215-enough-sleep.html).

[36] Christopher M. Barnes, "Sleep Well, Lead Better" *Harvard Business Review*, September-October 2018, pp.140–143.

[37] Alex M. Wood, et. al., "Gratitude Influences Sleep Through the Mechanism of Pre-Sleep Cognitions" *Journal of Psychosomatic Research*, Volume 66, Issue 1, January 2009, pp. 43-48 (DOI: https://doi.org/10.1016/j.jpsychores.2008.09.002).

Chapter 16: What Does Being Spiritual Mean?

[38] There are likely therapeutic horse ranches in your area, but I suggest Horse Spirit Connections (www.horsespiritconnections.com).

[39] Viktor E. Frankl, *Man's Search for Meaning* (Beacon Press, 1946).

Chapter 17: Your Need for Meaningful Connection

[40] Statistics Canada, "Study: Living Alone in Canada" in *The Daily* (March 6, 2019) (https://www150.statcan.gc.ca/n1/daily-quotidien/190306/dq190306b-eng.htm).

[41] *The Economist* and the Kaiser Family Foundation (KFF), "KFF/Economist Survey: One in Five Americans Report Always or Often Feeling Lonely or Socially Isolated, Frequently with Physical, Mental, and Financial Consequences" (August 31, 2018) (https://www.kff.org/other/press-release/survey-one-in-five-americans-report-loneliness-social-isolation/).

[42] Perlita Stroh, "Feeling Lonely? You're Not Alone – And It Could Be Affecting Your Physical Health" (CBC News, January 19, 2019), found at: https://www.cbc.ca/news/health/national-dealing-with-loneliness-1.4828017.

[43] Kerry Banks, "Loneliness: The Silent Killer" *University Affairs/Affaires Universitaires* magazine (Feb. 27, 2019) (https://www.universityaffairs.ca/features/feature-article/loneliness-the-silent-killer/).

[44] From the Canadian Mental Health Association website, "The Importance of Human Connection" (October 17, 2019) (https://cmha.ca/blogs/the-importance-of-human-connection/).

[45] *Ibid.*

Chapter 18: Has Your Spiritual Growth Become Stunted?

[46] Robert A. Emmons, Ph.D., *Thanks! How Practicing Gratitude Can Make You Happier* (New York, NY: Houghton Mifflin Harcourt Publishing Company, 2007).

Chapter 19: The Positive Impact of Mindfulness

[47] See: https://www.mindfulnessstudies.com/mindfulness/evidence/?gclid=CjwKCAjw34n5BRA9EiwA2u9k3z3Q8xGz55lwauxME0WZn8Tu5l9StleeAq-7YrzNswo39G1fHCA4WRoCengQAvD_BwE#_ftnref2

[48] A wonderful friend and colleague has written a book that guides individuals and organizations make conscious decisions when they contribute to their communities. The stories are profound and make you get clear about when, why, and how you maximize your meaning through sustainable contributions to the community. Check it out: Suzanne F. Stevens, *Make Your Contributions Count for You, Me, We: An Evolutionary Journey Inspired by the Wisdom of Pioneering African Women* (Collingwood, ON, 2020).

[49] Charlene Belitz and Meg Lundstrom, *The Power of Flow: Practical Ways to Transform Your Life with Meaningful Coincidence* (New York, NY: Three Rivers Press, 1998).

[50] You are welcome to enjoy my Playful Meditation for the Busy Mind (MP3). It can be accessed for free on my website: https://www.powerfuljourney.com/Resources.

[51] "I Hope You Dance" from *I Hope You Dance* (MCA Nashville, 2000).

[52] James Cameron (director), *Avatar* (20th Century Fox, 2009).

Chapter 20: Let Go, Let Joy In

[53] Melody Beattie, *The Language of Letting Go: Daily Meditations on Codependency* (Hazelden Publishing, 1990).

Bibliography

Anthony, Robert. *Beyond Positive Thinking: A No-Nonsense Formula for Getting the Results You Want* (Garden City, NY: Morgan James, 2004)

Banks, Kerry. "Loneliness: The Silent Killer" *University Affairs/Affaires Universitaires* magazine (Feb. 27, 2019) (https://www.universityaffairs.ca/features/feature-article/loneliness-the-silent-killer/)

Barnes, Christopher M. "Sleep Well, Lead Better" *Harvard Business Review*, September-October 2018, pp. 140–143

Beattie, Melody. *The Language of Letting Go: Daily Meditations on Codependency* (Hazelden Publishing, 1990)

Belitz, Charlene and Lundstrom, Meg. *The Power of Flow: Practical Ways to Transform Your Life with Meaningful Coincidence* (New York, NY: Three Rivers Press, 1998)

Brown, Brené. *Dare to Lead: Brave Work. Tough Conversations, Whole Hearts* (Random House, 2018)

—— *The Gifts of Imperfection: Let Go of Who You Think You're Supposed to Be and Embrace Who You Are* (Minnesota: Hazelden Publishing, 2010)

Cameron, James (director). *Avatar* (20th Century Fox, 2009)

Canadian Mental Health Association website, "The Importance of Human Connection" (October 17, 2019) (https://cmha.ca/blogs/the-importance-of-human-connection)

Canadian Society for Exercise Physiology, "Canadian Physical Activity Guidelines" found at: https://csep.ca/CMFiles/Guidelines/CSEP_PAGuidelines_0-65plus_en.pdf

Centers for Disease Control and Prevention, "1 in 3 Adults Don't Get Enough Sleep" (February 16, 2016) (https://www.cdc.gov/media/releases/2016/p0215-enough-sleep.html)

Centre for Addiction and Mental Health, "Workplace Mental Health: A Review and Recommendations" (January 2020): https://www.camh.ca/-/media/files/workplace-mental-health/workplacementalhealth-a-review-and-recommendations-pdf.pdf?la=en&hash=5B04D442283C004D0FF4A05E3662F39022268149

Cherry, Kendra. "How Multitasking Affects Productivity and Brain Health" (March 26, 2020) on verywellmind.com

Emmons, Robert A., Ph.D. *Thanks! How Practicing Gratitude Can Make You Happier* (New York, NY: Houghton Mifflin Harcourt Publishing Company, 2007)

Finley, Guy. *The Secret of Letting Go* (Llewellyn Publications, 2007)

Foundation for Inner Peace, *A Course in Miracles* (1975)

Fraenza, Christy B. "The Role of Social Influence in Anxiety and the Imposter Phenomenon" *Online Learning Journal* (June 2016) 20(2): 230-243 (DOI: http://dx.doi.org/10.24059/olj.v20i2.618)

Frankl, Viktor E. *Man's Search for Meaning* (Beacon Press, 1946)

Gamaiunova, Liudmila, et. al. "Exploration of Psychological Mechanisms of the Reduced Stress Response in Long-Term Meditation Practitioners" *Psychoneuroendocrinology*, volume 104 (June 2019), pp. 143-151

Harvard Health Publishing, "The Heart Attack Gender Gap" (April 2016): https://www.health.harvard.edu/heart-health/the-heart-attack-gender-gap

Harvard Press Release (December 18, 2019): "Close to half of U.S. population projected to have obesity by 2030" (https://www.hsph.harvard.edu/news/press-releases/half-of-us-to-have-obesity-by-2030/)

Hay, Louise. *You Can Heal Your Life* (Hay House Inc., 1984)

Hendricks, Gay. *The Big Leap: Conquer Your Hidden Fear and Take Life to the Next Level* (New York, NY: Harper Collins, 2009)

Hollis, James. *Living an Examined Life: Wisdom for the Second Half of the Journey* (Boulder, CO: Sounds True Inc., 2018)

Larson, Lila. *Small Business, Big Growth: 50 Ways to Get Clear, Get Focused and Get Better Results* (Winnipeg, MB, 2015)

Leech, Joe. "7 Science-Based Health Benefits of Drinking Enough Water" (June 30, 2020) on Healthline.com (https://www.healthline.com/nutrition/7-health-benefits-of-water)

Lencioni, Patrick. *The 5 Dysfunctions of a Team: A Leadership Fable* (Jossey-Bass, 2002)

Maté, Gabor. *When the Body Says No: The Cost of Hidden Stress* (Toronto: Vintage Canada, 2003)

Meyers, Nancy (director). *The Holiday* (Columbia Pictures, 2006)

Ophir, Eyal; Nass, Clifford; and Wagner, Anthony D. "Cognitive Control in Media Multitaskers." *Proceedings of the National Academy of Sciences of the United States of America* (September 15, 2009) 106 (37): 15583-15587 (https://doi.org/10.1073/pnas.0903620106)

Piedmont Healthcare, "What Your Stool Says About Your Health" (https://www.piedmont.org/living-better/what-your-stool-says-about-your-health)

Statistics Canada, "Study: Living Alone in Canada" in *The Daily* (March 6, 2019) (https://www150.statcan.gc.ca/n1/daily-quotidien/190306/dq190306b-eng.htm)

Stevens, Suzanne F. *Make Your Contributions Count for You, Me, We: An Evolutionary Journey Inspired by the Wisdom of Pioneering African Women* (Collingwood, ON, 2020)

Stroh, Perlita. "Feeling Lonely? You're Not Alone – And It Could Be Affecting Your Physical Health" (CBC News, January 19, 2019), found at: https://www.cbc.ca/news/health/national-dealing-with-loneliness-1.4828017

The Economist and the Kaiser Family Foundation (KFF), "KFF/Economist Survey: One in Five Americans Report Always or Often Feeling Lonely or Socially Isolated, Frequently with Physical, Mental, and Financial Consequences" (August 31, 2018) (https://www.kff.org/other/press-release/survey-one-in-five-americans-report-loneliness-social-isolation/)

The Heart and Stroke Foundation of Canada at www.heartandstroke.ca

Twells, Laurie K., Ph.D., et. al. "Current and Predicted Prevalence of Obesity in Canada: A Trend Analysis" CMAL Open March 3, 2014, vol. 2, no. 1, pp. E18-E26 (DOI: 10.9778/cmajo.20130016)

Wilson, James. L. *Adrenal Fatigue: The 21st Century Stress Syndrome* (Smart Publications, 2001)

Womack, Lee Ann. "I Hope You Dance" from *I Hope You Dance* (MCA Nashville, 2000)

Wood, Alex M., et. al. "Gratitude Influences Sleep Through the Mechanism of Pre-Sleep Cognitions" *Journal of Psychosomatic Research*, Volume 66, Issue 1, January 2009, pp. 43-48 (DOI: https://doi.org/10.1016/j.jpsychores.2008.09.002)

What's Next?

How Cate Can Help You or Your Organization

Purchase this book for each of your team members to recognize hard work and effort!

COME AND PLAY WITH CATE:

- Book a Discovery Session with Cate: admin@powerfuljourney.com
- Get Cate's free "Playful Meditation for the Busy Mind"
- Join Cate's monthly vlog

GET MORE POWERHOUSE FROM CATE:

- Complete Your Leadership Audit to clarify your or your organization's needs for resiliency
- Get Cate's Four-Room Checklist
- Do the online quiz
- Attend one of Cate's "BE the Leading Lady in Your Own Life" retreats
- Learn more about Cate's other powerhouse resources

BOOK CATE:

- For a powerful training session – one-on-one or leadership group
- To facilitate your next transformative team or leadership retreat
- For your inspirational keynote address

CONTACT CATE:

www.powerfuljourney.com

www.linkedin.com/in/catecollins

www.facebook.com/Cate Collins/

www.instagram.com/PowerfulCate

www.youtube.com/channel/UC7iRTJ10Cm1qcs|OpU8P33Q

About the Author

Cate Collins is a passionate international speaker, trainer, retreat facilitator, author of several effective resources, and CEO of Powerful Journey Consulting. She helps leaders and their teams loosen their underwear so they can be the best version of themselves.

Like many ambitious people, Cate lived most of her life striving, achieving, and being there for others, while ignoring her own needs. Suffering a serious burnout several years ago made her recognize her mistakes and stoked her desire to help others avoid the same fate. First-hand observation of her colleagues and herself, showed her how easy it is to hide yourself in busyness, work, and service to others, rather than deal head-on with personal issues such as grief, divorce, toxic work environments, or trauma.

Cate has a seasoned background in behavioural science as a mental health counsellor, leadership coach, and was one of the youngest executive directors of a not-for-profit in Canada. A member of the Canadian Association of Professional Speakers, Cate was hand-picked to train with Jack Canfield, coauthor of the New York Times Bestselling *Chicken Soup for the Soul*® series and *The Success Principles: How to Get from Where You Are to Where You Want to Be*™.

Her Four Room Success Framework provides simple and impactful strategies to develop resilient leaders, create healthier cultures, and build engaged teams to minimize workplace conflict, mental health issues, miscommunication, sick leaves, and improve the quality of their lives.

For over 20 years, Cate has facilitated customized teambuilding, resiliency, and mindfulness retreats for health care, not-for-profit organizations, government agencies, funeral associations, the United States Army and businesses worldwide. She hosted two retreats in beautiful Costa Rica and Arizona where she hired therapeutic horse facilities. Her powerful, year-long leadership program includes quarterly leadership retreats.

Cate is committed to supporting her community and especially local shelters and organizations who support the needs of children and youth. She is a bit of a "health nut" who teaches Pilates and stays abreast of current health research.

The best way of dealing with leadership burnout is to prevent it in the first place. Leaders and teams need real strategies and techniques to overcome their internal obstacles and build a healthier workplace for themselves and others. Cate's life's purpose is to remind people who they are and provide them with strategies to own their power to make that happen. Everyone deserves a powerful journey.